Startup Patterns
How Great Startup Teams Work

Sam McAfee

Sam McAfee

ISBN: 1536947784
ISBN-13: 978-1536947786

DEDICATION

For Angelina, without whom I could not have done this work.

Sam McAfee

CONTENTS

Sam McAfee

ACKNOWLEDGMENTS

I received a great deal of support and encouragement from so many people while creating this book.

A big thanks first to Donald Reinertsen, the unparalleled champion of lean product development, whose work inspired me to write this book.

My colleagues at Neo Innovation, where I worked when I first started on this journey, gave me the push I needed to take the first few steps. David Bland, Peter Shanley, Jonathan Irwin, and Giff Constable, all contributed ideas and feedback that were indispensable in finding the right tone, content, and direction for the book. David Trejo, Gon Zifroni, Fei Fang, and the rest of the team at Neo were also very supportive.

I am deeply grateful to the startup founders who I interviewed for the book, some of whom are referenced within, and a great many more who graciously shared stories that I have woven into the lessons that I present here. I wholeheartedly thank Kyle Wild and Lisa Neilsen at KeenIO, Ashii Vel at Traveling Spoon, Rob Fan and Rob Slifke at Sharethrough, Sonya Green, Jonathan McCoy, and Renee Teeley for sharing stories and comments that appear in the text. I also owe thanks to these startup leaders for help in shaping the content (in no particular order): Hilary Weber, Eoin Dowling, Joe Johnston, Peter Arvai, Corey Lydstone, Jeff Barrett, Andrea Ballerini, Mark Abramson, Claire Hough, Lindsay Nelson.

A big thanks to Alex Roman for working with me on so many iterations of the cover design.

But most of all, I could never have finished this project without the love, support, encouragement, feedback, and guidance of my loving wife, Angelina, and two boys, Isaac and Malcolm.

PROLOGUE

Hang around Silicon Valley for any length of time and you'll hear plenty of opinions about what it takes to be a successful entrepreneur.

A decent number of those opinions will include some depiction of "a little bit crazy." People who leave their day job to start their own company would have to be just a little bit off their rocker, wouldn't they?

Some suggest that this risk-taking is what makes entrepreneurs think so differently about the world. That it enables them to visualize amazing new innovations and successfully bring them to market.

Maybe so.

To be sure, entrepreneurship is not for the faint-hearted. Companies are incredibly hard things to build, and most don't survive beyond the first year. There are so many things to do in a startup, and so many things that can go wrong, that it is kind of amazing that any survive at all.

But some do. In nearly all cases of success, the founding team faced hurdles right from the start, any one of which could have killed the venture. If you buy the Silicon Valley mythology, there is often a visionary founder that motivates the team through the endless slog of trial and error.

We celebrate this mythos of the wild-eyed startup founder in Silicon Valley. The cafes and restaurants echo with stories of the heroic entrepreneur, their legendary eccentricities or obsessive-compulsive behaviors. It was they who saw what others couldn't and steered their team through innumerable minefields to finally reach success. Steve Jobs may be the most famous example, but he is by no means the only incarnation of the mad tortured-genius entrepreneur.

But there is a little more to it than just that.

The mythology of entrepreneurship leaves out a lot of critical detail about how startups actually work in the real world. The most stark difference between myth and reality is that great products are always built by teams, not individuals. It is the painstaking execution of the vision by a great team that makes the real difference between success and failure.

This is a book about teamwork.

Look at the startup products and teams that have been successful. There are patterns of activity, organization, and attitude that are consistent in nearly every case. These patterns are difficult to see from the outside, because they don't make for sexy "Tech Crunch" stories. But these patterns are far more responsible for the success or failure of a startup than the sideshow antics of any single founder.

The patterns practiced by world-class startup teams are observable. From the seemingly chaotic background noise of startup life, we can define and generalize them for use by other teams. Following these patterns dramatically improves those teams' chances of creating world-class products themselves. Indeed, the consistently successful execution of product development teams is neither magic nor accident.

That is not to say you can build smart, innovative products with execution alone. Indeed, it is critical that the team is able to execute against a greater vision in order to build a truly successful company. Without a clear vision and strong leadership, even solid execution leads to products and services that feel hollow or shallow. Most literature on entrepreneurship is about the vision, creativity, and leadership side. Very little exists on practical, day-to-day execution. This book is intended to bridge that gap.

In what follows, I attempt to illustrate a series of reusable organization and workflow patterns. These are patterns that successful startup product teams use either consciously or not. My goal was to combine the principles from methods like Agile and Lean Startup with practical examples of those principles in action. I hope thus to give the reader a good head start in establishing their own product development process.

So let's dive in…

1. VISION THROUGH UNCERTAINTY

It is unusually warm for a November day in the San Francisco Bay Area, when I meet with Kyle Wild near his office in San Francisco's South of Market district. Kyle is cofounder and CEO of Keen IO, a fast-growing tech startup that offers a general purpose event data platform for developers. We've bumped into each other here and there around the startup scene for a few years. He's one of the first people I thought of when I decided to write this book.

We are sitting with our artisan coffees, sharing a bench in a bizarre little post-modern parklet nestled between the Deloitte skyscraper and the massive, multi-block construction site of what will soon be the SF Transbay terminal. The young maple trees are delicately and yet somehow forcefully arranged in rows between the hard angled dark wood and brushed steel benches. Over Kyle's shoulder is a multicolored piece of abstract modern art, comprising several pixelated manifestations of the mouse pointer icon. It seems a fitting location for this conversation.

I am listening to Kyle recount the early origins of his company, which he founded with his two best friends. Keen's product has a rapidly growing following among the throng of tech startups cropping up all the time in SF. He's just finished telling me that the idea for the product emerged out of their observations of developer needs while in previous roles, two founders having come from Salesforce's force.com team, the other from Google's analytics team. The product is a developer tool, so the go-to-market strategy necessarily required a lot of direct developer relations, some solid documentation, and a never ending stream of feature requests.

"So, how did you guys balance the pressure of releasing an early MVP with the sheer technical complexity of what you were building for the long-term?"

"To be honest," he says, "we aren't really big fans of Lean Startup. At least, not if you're trying to build something big, technical, and generalizable."

I try hard not to betray any emotion on my face as I absorb this statement. I'm pretty severely committed to the principle of releasing early and adjusting your product based on feedback from the market. What Kyle is saying though makes me think hard about those principles. I respect him, so I listen carefully to what he says next.

"You see, there is a local maxima problem with Lean Startup. The methods encourage you to find a signal wherever you can, and then iterate toward it. The fastest way for us to get traction early on might have been to pick a single vertical, say marketing or financial tools, and build mainly for that market, only extending to adjacent use cases later on. If we had made a tool like that, say a marketing analytics dashboard, and got positive feedback from the market that we were on to something, lean says that we should double down in that vertical.

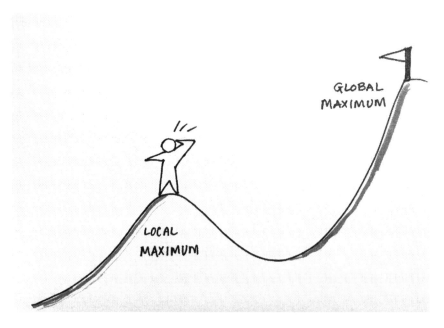

Figure 1. A local maximum can fool you into thinking you've got the best solution.

He sips from his cup, then continues. I'm not sure I agree, but I am intrigued with his reasoning.

"We always knew we wanted to build a general data platform that would be useful in any vertical. We fiercely resisted the temptation to build yet another platform for marketers or product managers. What we were trying to do was much harder. And it took a lot longer. We almost didn't make it."

As he finishes that sentence, it starts raining, and we start looking around for some shelter.

The interviews I conducted for this book, like this one with Kyle, were mostly with personal contacts from the startup community in SF, or folks who were referred to me by those people. It is thus by no means an unbiased or "statistically significant" study. These are people that I knew personally, or at least knew about, and reached out to them intentionally for an interview. Nevertheless, in most cases I had not made contact in a few years and I had really no idea what I would learn about how their companies were operating when I finally sat down with them and asked about it. So it was both validating and not a little surprising to find patterns and themes emerging over and over in these conversations with founders.

The theme Kyle was touching on here, in particular, struck me as so significant and far-reaching that I'll set it out for you right at the beginning of this book. There is an apparent tension between the adherence to a vision of a world-changing company, a characteristic that we may associate with a Steve Jobs-style approach to company-building, and the methodically tactical day-to-day experimentation of the Build-Measure-Learn loop popularized by The Lean Startup book. This apparent paradox between sticking to a long-term vision, on the one hand, and following iterative methods to discover a new business model, on the other, came up in at least half the interviews as something many entrepreneurs struggle with. For now, I just want to present this apparent contradiction as a framing for our discussion.

Under nearby shelter, Kyle picks up the thread where we left it.

"Everyone wanted us to build a dashboard or some other custom set of features that would be specific to their industry. But that would have distracted us from building something much more fundamental, and ultimately I think more valuable."

2. CONNECTING YOUR VISION TO THE PRESENT

Startups are often assumed to be the purest form, the very essence, of innovation. But that is a fundamental misunderstanding of startups. To be innovative requires rethinking existing markets, products, customer segments, and value propositions in radically new ways. Precious few startups do anything close to that.

Well, yours does, of course! Your startup's one of the good ones.

I'm a huge proponent of Lean Startup and Agile. Much of this book will reference practices and principles from those powerful sister methodologies. Some of it will be familiar to you, while some may be totally new.

But there's a tension between vision and execution. In the last section, Kyle helped us realize that simply iterating based on market feedback, without a strong vision, will not get you where you need to go.

For now then, let's acknowledge that there is an apparent paradox between having a big long term vision, and developing your company with an iterative, data-driven process like Agile and Lean Startup. How do we bridge the gap between these two essential aspects of building startups?

It would be useful if we had a tool that allowed us to describe our vision, broken down into its constituent components, in such a way that we could then systematically test those components with real data. It turns out there is such a tool. It's called the Business Model Canvas.

There's been enough written about the canvas elsewhere that I won't extol its virtues right here. Suffice it to say using a canvas is pretty much table stakes for startups these days.

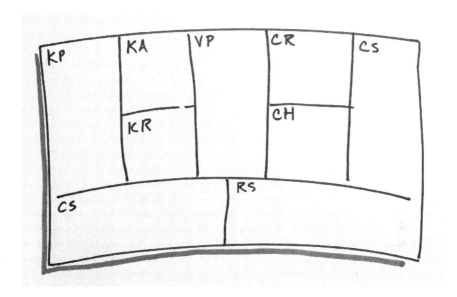

Figure 2. The Business Model Canvas is like a one-page business plan.

But how does the business model canvas enable you to bridge the gap between Lean Startup product validation and adhering to a long-term vision?

The beauty of the canvas is that it divides an overall business model into nine generalizable pieces that apply across all business models. That means you can be wrong about one of the components, such as your distribution channel, or key partners, etc., and still be right about all the other components.

It also means that you can test aspects of your business model in isolation, while keeping the other aspects relatively constant. Assuming you're applying the scientific method of course!

And it means that you can model other people's businesses, such as the huge incumbents in an industry that you want to break into, or smaller competitors that are already operating in that industry, in order to better understand how to position your new venture.

Let's look at some specifics from the enterprise world.

In the seminal corporate strategy book, the Alchemy of Growth, we are taught that Horizon One initiatives represent the current businesses operated by the corporation. Horizon Two initiatives are those that expand current initiatives into new adjacent markets, or offer enhanced value propositions to existing customers. This is sometimes referred to as incremental innovation.

Horizon Three initiatives are those that diverge radically from the day-to-day operations of the existing corporation, seeking entirely different business models in new and emerging markets. These are typically the same opportunities that would be chased by competing startup companies, like yours.

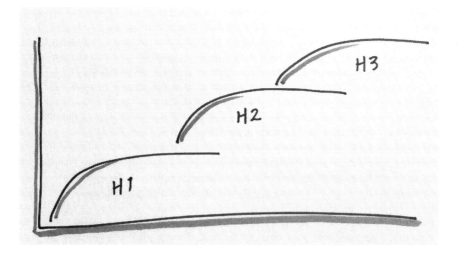

Figure 3. The horizon model illustrates the three types of innovation, and their focuses.

The three horizons for growth concept illustrates how companies can manage their current product lines and businesses while simultaneously seeking innovation in new products, businesses, or markets.

Applying the business model canvas to the Horizon framework illuminates a few interesting insights. First, we can say that in an existing Horizon One business the entire business model canvas is well understood. Next, we can see that a Horizon Two initiative might only be seeking to change one or two components from the business model canvas, such as the Customer Segment or the Value Proposition.

But a Horizon Three initiative for a modern corporation is likely to differ from their main business model by both Customer Segment and Value Proposition at least. Probably, Channel, Revenue, and Key Activities are also different. This is what makes Horizon Three initiatives both exciting and risky for corporations.

Why is it relevant to understand corporate models for growth when you're working on a startup? Well, put simply, they are trying to capture the same opportunities that you are. So you would do well to pay attention to what they're doing.

Creating a truly innovative startup, it's highly likely that their Horizon Three is the area where you are playing as well. That's because if your focus is an innovation that's effectively a Horizon Two initiative for a large competitor, you are unlikely to win sufficient market share to survive and grow before they come along and crush you. Horizon Two initiatives are just too easy for big companies to capture since it's just an extension of their core capabilities.

But Horizon Three is dangerous waters for big companies. And it's where startups really excel!

Later in the book we discuss dealing with competitors. You may find it useful for now to think about your competitors being not other startups, but rather large incumbents who are exploring their Horizon Two and Three options.

Now let's apply this thinking to our apparent paradox, the tension between a big vision in an experiment-focused development process.

Recall our conversation from the last section with Kyle, on KeenIO and their original vision. With the business model canvas and Horizon Three thinking in mind, one can easily see how the difference between a niche marketing dashboard and a generalizable data platform would be simple to express on a canvas. The customer segments are different. The value proposition is different. The channels, key partners, resources, and activities are different. Heck, the whole business model is different!

If Kyle and his cofounders had blindly followed lean startup methods without having a vision–and many companies do just that–they would have ended up building a business that was much smaller and less sustainable.

Further, there were many more larger players in the marketing and analytics spaces at the time of their founding than there were in general event data processing tools. I didn't ask Kyle specifically about competition per se, but it was clear that he and his cofounders envisioned something that was not simply an adjacent feature set for an existing platform.

So you have your business model canvas all filled out, right? In fact, why don't you go ahead and do that now? Don't worry–I'll wait.

Look at the customer segments and value proposition boxes. How many other tools, products, and services currently attempt to serve that customer with a similar value proposition?

If your aren't sure, when you get to the chapter on solving the right problem, I'll show you some practical steps to find out.

For now, let's assume that you've identified a customer segment that is not currently being served by a strong incumbent, and you have a value proposition that isn't already covered by existing tools and services.

It's a good start. But the revenue model, specifically the unit economics of your business, could be the key area that makes or breaks your startup.

Let's turn our attention to startup economics, and see how your model can avoid the most common traps.

3. ECONOMIC FRAMEWORKS

Building a new product is inherently a creative endeavor. It requires immense vision, imagination, even artistry. We don't think of startups as being within the artistic domains, typically. Yet, good products are certainly the result of, at a minimum, good design (visual design as well as systems design) and expert craftsmanship in the implementation of that design.

There is a lot more to it, of course. But without a strong creative vision, there isn't much to work with. Every one of the founders I talked with for this book—and in fact, quite probably all founders I have worked with in my career whom I would consider even a little bit successful—have each had in common a very high degree of creativity.

And yet building a product company is inherently an economic endeavor, firmly rooted in the domain of mathematics and accounting, and more recently, in science. You cannot be successful as a startup without a very strong foundation in general business practices. Even if your true passion is the creative side of product design and development, it is essential to ground your product development activities in a well-defined economic framework.

This is certainly true for Aashi Vel, co-founder of Traveling Spoon, a marketplace that allows travelers to book food-related experiences at the homes of locals across Asia. These experiences can be a home cooked meal, a cooking class, or a guided tour of the local market. I met Aashi and her co-founder Stephanie Lawrence about two years ago when the marketplace was still just an MVP website intended to measure the demand side of their marketplace. By the time we spoke again recently about economic frameworks, Traveling Spoon had already grown significantly, hiring several new team members and striking deals with a few key partner networks.

You don't have to be a trained CPA or MBA to develop this framework. You just need a basic understanding of the principles of running a business. You'll account for your costs and revenues, and you'll attempt to calculate the impact of different actions you might take on your bottom line (which is likely profit, or perhaps revenue in the very beginning). Having an economic framework then enables you to make prioritization decisions based on the overall economic outcomes from those decisions.

Figure 4. You can't improve what you don't measure.

About the importance of building an economic model early on in their startup process, Aashi agreed emphatically. Very early on, pretty much at the idea phase, the two founders began quantifying as much of the market information as they could find. The looked at the overall size of the travel market, they estimated the typical annual spend on travel-related experiences for their target demographic, and they carefully examined the competitive landscape for comparable products and services. All this put together gave them a sense of whether their idea had a reasonable chance at becoming a large and successful business.

Once that understanding was in place, the team needed data on the demand for their particular solution idea, both in terms of the volume of demand and the price sensitivity of potential customers, as well as the cost of acquiring potential hosts and matching them with travelers. They used a range of techniques to collect this data, including an MVP website to measure the demand side, and visits to India and Thailand to seek out and interview prospective hosts. But throughout all of this, they continually updated and refined their economic model, adjusting their assumptions accordingly whenever new data required it.

I asked Aashi what mistakes could have been made had they not been so rigorous with their economic model.

"How do you know how much cash you have on hand, at any given time, for starters" she asked in response?

"When you need to make decisions about whether to hire a new team member, or when to raise money, or whether to outsource part of your production system, you have to know the financial effects such decisions will have. At a minimum, you have to have an accurate sense of cash flow just to function on a daily basis."

It seemed obvious hearing Aashi put it like this. But I can't tell you how may startup founders I have bluntly asked exactly about cash flow projections only to get blank stares in reply.

"A more complicated example," she went on, "is if you're considering a partnership for some part of your business model, such as customer acquisition in our case. We work with tour operators to help us identify and acquire travelers who might be interested in our food experiences. You need to be able to understand very precisely what the benefit of the partnership is going to be in terms of raw numbers of customers acquired through that channel, and exactly what it will cost you to acquire them through this deal. Without a model, you can make very serious errors in these calculations."

4. CHOOSING METRICS FOR SAAS PRODUCTS

When it comes to metrics, there are two types of founders that I meet on a regular basis. One type is not using any metrics at all, feverishly building a company seemingly on guesswork and hunches. When prodded about this, they always seem to understand the importance of metrics. They usually just don't know where to get started.

The other type is drowning in data, surrounded by dashboards and detailed projections in spreadsheets all day long. They behave more like a data magpie, ceaselessly jumping from one minute measurement to another, but never able to construct an overall picture of their progress.

Ironically, both of these extremes have the same problem. They lack just the right amount of data to make informed business decisions.

The Internet is ringing with articles about the importance of data, and tactical approaches to measuring customer behavior or perform conversion-rate optimization. Unfortunately, most of these articles assume that you've properly set up an economic framework for your business already, so that you can take advantage of the tactics they are imparting to you.

I am going to assume just the opposite. I am going to assume you need me to start at the beginning and walk you through it step by step.

The metrics work that I prepare with clients combines two popular frameworks. The first is presented in Lean Analytics, by Ben Yoskovitz and Allistair Croll. The second, so-called "Pirate Metrics", was popularized by veteran venture capitalist, Dave McClure.

I have found that combining the two frameworks can give you clear insights into which metrics you need to be focused on at which stages of your company's development.

First let's look at the two frameworks separately.

Lean Analytics Stages

The Lean Analytics book talks about three stages of the startup lifecycle (actually, there are more than three, but these are the three that matter for our purposes): the Empathy stage, the Stickiness stage, and the Growth stage.

In the Empathy stage, a startup is concerned with answering the questions:

"How well do we know our customers? Are we solving the right problem, a painful problem that most if not all of our customers experience regularly?".

In the Stickiness stage, a startup is concerned with answering the question:

"Is the solution we are offering solving the problem to a sufficient degree that customers will come back and use it again, or purchase more additional products from us?"

In the Growth stage, a startup is concerned with answering the question:

"How can we make our solution so good that our customers rave about it to their friends and colleagues?"

Why do these stages matter to us when we are building a startup?

Because if you are still unclear about the answer to the questions in the Empathy stage, it is totally inappropriate to worry about measurements that would be targeting the Growth stage. Until you are sure that you are solving a real problem in a way that delivers value to your customers, you need to spend your effort on that before moving to the next stage.

Keep those stages in mind; we'll come back to them in a moment.

Metrics for Pirates

A few years ago, Dave McClure blew minds and won hearts by presenting startup metrics through the lens of a sales funnel. He whimsically coined these Pirate Metrics. It certainly expanded my perspective.

Basically, these are metrics categories, rather than specific measurements, that correspond to the customer lifecycle (as opposed to the startup lifecycle above). The customer proceeds through a series of stages with regard to their awareness of, and passion for, your product.

Acquisition

Getting users from some marketing channel to arrive on your website and interact with your product in some way counts as acquisition. Opinions differ about exactly when you count someone as "acquired". Experts I have discussed this with in digital marketing usually say that bounced traffic doesn't count. A user is only acquired if they stick around a little and consume some content or make a minimal contribution to the experience.

Activation

This set of metrics will be unique to every product. It's typically an action that indicates some level of emotional commitment to the product, such as a sign up for a free trial, a comment or up-vote, or subscribing to a mailing list. It usually involves giving some personal information, such as an email address. But it may even count as a full purchase, depending on your model.

Retention

Customers are hopefully so delighted with your service that they continue their subscription, or come back and buy more organic tofu from your online vegan superstore. Whatever your core value proposition, these metrics capture repeat or ongoing business. The inverse of retention, by the way, is called "churn".

Revenue

This is usually something simple like overall revenue earned per customer. It can sometimes be more complicated if your business model is a marketplace or a social / content platform and you need to earn revenue from a second stakeholder. In any case, you'll have some measure of recurring revenue.

Referral

These metrics track the acquisition of new customers by referral from existing customers. This can include segments of users who were acquired from a referral, and it may include measures of users' sharing behaviors within a particular product experience, that would then result in new users coming in from those shared bits of content.

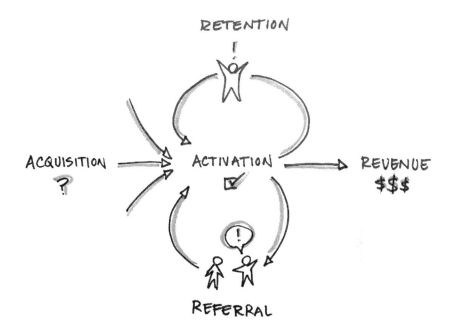

Figure 5. David Bland taught me to represent Pirate Metrics graphically like this.

Now, Lean on your Pirates

Let's mix the two frameworks now:

In the Empathy stage, you are usually measuring Acquisition and Activation. Does your value proposition and marketing channels, which you wrote on your business model canvas, lead to a successful new customer sign-up?

If so, you may in fact understand your customer and offer something they want.

In the Stickiness stage, you are looking at Retention. Did your solution provide enough value, relieve the suffering or provide the joy, that made your customers come back for more? You are probably also now measuring Revenue. Are you making enough money (LTV) to justify the Acquisition channels and methods (CAC) that you're using?

In the Growth stage, you are finally concerned with Referrals. Does your product or service rock your customers' worlds to the extent that they simply can't stop telling all their friends about it?

A SaaS P&L

If you are building a modern Software-as-a-Service product, you can represent your economic model in a simple spreadsheet format that follows the basics of a standard Profit & Loss table (any MBAs out there? No? Good, they always raise their hands and ask annoying questions at this point).

Take a look at this structure.

	A	B	C	D	E	F	G	H	I	J	K	L	M
	Month	Jan	Feb	Mar	Apr	May	Jun	Jul	Aug	Sep	Oct	Nov	Dec
2	Total Traffic	0.00	0.00	50,000.00	60,000.00	72,000.00	86,400.00	103,680.00	124,416.00	149,299.20	179,159.04	214,990.85	257,989.02
3	Conversion	3.00%	3.00%	3.00%	3.00%	3.00%	3.00%	3.00%	3.00%	3.00%	3.00%	3.00%	3.00%
4	New Members	0.00	0.00	1,500.00	1,800.00	2,160.00	2,592.00	3,110.40	3,732.48	4,478.98	5,374.77	6,449.73	7,739.67
5	Existing Members	0.00	0.00	0.00	1,200.00	2,400.00	3,848.00	4,992.00	6,481.92	8,171.52	10,120.40	12,396.13	15,076.69
6	Retention	0.80	0.80	0.80	0.80	0.80	0.80	0.80	0.80	0.80	0.80	0.80	0.80
7	Members	0.00	0.00	1,200.00	2,400.00	3,848.00	4,992.00	6,481.92	8,171.52	10,120.40	12,396.13	15,076.69	18,263.09
8	Subscription Price	$25.00	$25.00	$25.00	$25.00	$25.00	$25.00	$25.00	$25.00	$25.00	$25.00	$25.00	$25.00
9	Sales Revenue	$0.00	$0.00	$30,000.00	$60,000.00	$91,200.00	$124,800.00	$162,048.00	$204,288.00	$253,009.92	$309,903.36	$376,917.20	$456,327.17
10													
11													
12	Fixed Costs	$5,000	$5,000	$5,000	$5,000	$5,000	$5,000	$5,000	$5,000	$5,000	$5,000	$5,000	$5,000
13	Labor	$38,000	$38,000	$36,000	$36,000	$36,000	$36,000	$36,000	$36,000	$36,000	$36,000	$36,000	$36,000
14	Ad Costs	$0	$0	$25,000	$30,000	$36,000	$43,200	$51,840	$62,208	$74,650	$89,580	$107,495	$128,995
15	Variable Costs	$36,000	$36,000	$61,000	$66,000	$72,000	$79,200	$87,840	$98,208	$110,650	$125,580	$143,495	$164,995
16	Total Costs	$41,000	$41,000	$66,000	$71,000	$77,000	$84,200	$92,840	$103,208	$115,650	$130,580	$148,495	$169,995
17	Operating Profit	(41,000)	(41,000)	(36,000)	(11,000)	14,200	40,800	69,208	101,080	137,360	179,324	228,422	286,333
18	Cumulative Profit	(41,000)	(82,000)	(118,000)	(129,000)	(114,800)	(74,200)	(4,992)	96,088	233,448	412,772	641,194	927,527

Figure 6. Screenshot of a fictional SaaS product pro forma income model.

You have columns extending from left to right in units of time. Weeks and months are pretty typical. If you're in a huge company, maybe you use quarters.

The first several rows list out all of the stages necessary to acquire, activate, retain, and earn revenue from a customer. There rows further down (I like a visual whitespace break to keep it clean) reflect your operating and development costs.

The last two rows simply add the costs and revenues together, and arrive at a profit (or loss) for the time period, as well as a running cumulative total profit (or loss). You can see in this example, we lose about $130k before climbing back up to break even in August. By year's end, we're close to a million in cumulative revenue and growing quickly. This is, of course, a fictional example. But you get the idea.

Next, Putting It Together

In the following section, we're going to look at how to apply a Lean Startup and Agile approach to using experiments to validate our business model.

5. THE VALUE OF INFORMATION

In Lean Startup jargon, we talk about the Build-Measure-Learn loop. It is an iterative process to validate assumptions you have about your business. The basic idea is that you build your product in small pieces. You release it continuously to potential customers and measure their response to it. Gradually you adapt your product based on that feedback.

The reason this process works at all is because of the value of information. The value of a piece information is the amount you would be willing to pay for it to make a business decision based on it. But how does that relate to product development? Let's take a closer look.

All business is about taking risks. You invest time or money in something you plan to sell in the market. You do so hoping that you can make your investment back plus a little bit extra. It doesn't matter if you were financing a trade voyage in the fourteenth century, or you are building a new technology product today. All business activity is about either making the product or service or delivering it to customers. All business decisions are about finding ways to mitigate the risk of doing so. The way to mitigate risk is to gather information that would affect your investment.

Risk, then, is a *quantitative* thing. It is an amount of loss you might suffer, times the probability that such a loss will happen. Risk can be calculated assuming you can quantify those two components. Information is valuable only insofar as it enables you to make a business decision. If you can reduce uncertainty, you can reduce risk, even if you have little or no control over the amount of a possible loss.

Got that? Even if the amount of a loss is fixed, you can still reduce risk by increasing your information about its likelihood.

And if risk can be calculated, opportunities to reduce it can also be quantified. Think of it like insurance. The whole Build-Measure-Learn loop is in essence as an abstract kind of insurance. You pay for new information to reduce your risks. What you pay is your cost of running the loop process itself, the building, the measuring, and the learning.

The tricky thing about insurance is that we should never pay more for it than the loss it covers. So your loop should be generating more information value than the cost of iterating itself. How do you know if you're doing this? It depends on the complexity of your business model.

Your economic framework will be as simple or as complex as your business model. If you are in a tech startup, your business model will have a certain degree of complexity to it. Your initial phases of development can be far removed from realizing any actual revenue. This is definitely the case with multi-sided markets or technology platforms. It is likely you'll have some serious calculations to do to forecast your likely revenue or profitability. The more complicated those calculations, the more risky they are.

Let's look at a concrete example of information value in action. Suppose you are building a platform for buyers and sellers of something (Toasters? Classic cars? Whatever). Suppose your economic framework shows exactly how many of these transactions you need per month in order for your company to break even. And suppose your website processes far fewer than that. You're effectively losing money every week. Maybe you got some funding early on, but it's going to run out unless you crack this soon.

You have a short list of ideas for how to increase the number of transactions on the site. Maybe bringing in more buyers through various buyer-related features and incentives. Maybe fiddling with the transaction fees sellers pay you to use the site, or other aspects of the payment infrastructure. Still others involve various conversion optimization hacks of the selling process itself. You only have capacity to run one experiment at a time (maybe it's just you and a partner or co-founder). How do you decide which one to try first?

You run the experiment with the highest business value. The experiment with the highest business value reduces uncertainty around the highest risk assumption. Like the risk that you will not process any transactions on the site this month.

I know what you're thinking. "Great, Sam. But how do I quantify that?!"

OK, OK. Let's do it.

Again, you have to have a reasonably thorough economic framework in place to do these calculations. In our marketplace example, you would need to model the on-boarding funnel for both buyer and seller accounts. You would have some idea of how many buyers and sellers you need to transact business to hit your revenue targets. Assuming you're charging a fee for each sale, you've already got a total number of sales transactions as a target to hit each month or week.

Next, you need to plug into the model any actual data you have. Use existing traffic on the site or the past months of transaction data. Whatever you can scrape together from your progress so far will help. You can look at each conversion step in those funnels and calculate a rate. If you had 100 buyers land on your site, and only 10 started browsing, well, that's a 10% conversion for that step. If for every 10 browsing buyers, only 2 buys something, that's 20% of browsers, and 2% of overall traffic. If each transaction is $100, and you charge a 3% transaction fee on top of that, you make $3.00 per transaction. Each buyer that lands on the site has a 2% likelihood of spending $100 and earning you $3, and is thus worth 2% of $3 to you, or $0.06.

Meanwhile, maybe you had 20 sellers list products this month, and 4 of them sold them through the site. That's a 20% conversion from listing a product to selling it, and netting you a transaction fee. So, each seller that lists a product is worth 20% of $3, or $0.60.

Figure 7. Risk is quantifiable by multiplying expected loss by probability of occurrence.

You probably notice a major difference in the relative importance of features for sellers versus buyers. Sellers, at least those that list products, are worth 10x what a buyer is worth in terms of contributing to your revenue. Now let's drive this home.

One experiment may increase the conversion from a browsing buyer to a purchaser. Another experiment may increase a seller's likelihood to make a sale. The former would have to move the needle 10 times higher than the latter in order to be even equal for consideration. Chances of that extremely slim.

Put another way, the information content in any experiment on the buyer's funnel is relatively low. Compared to information we'd gain by running experiments on the seller's side, it pales in comparison. Of course, to have a successful marketplace, we need to pay attention to both. But these calculations can help us focus where we will get the most bang for our buck in running experiments.

Our economic framework and a fun traffic and sales scenario illustrated the information value in experiments. In a later chapter, we're going to talk about how to integrate this knowledge into the development process more generally. But first, we need to build the product team.

6. COFOUNDERS, HIRING, AND OUTSOURCING

Entrepreneurship is extraordinarily hard. You may not want to go it alone.

Some founders are able to build significant businesses by themselves. You do see Software-as-a-Service products these days that are built, owned, and operated by a single individual, usually someone with both tech and marketing skills.

Renee Teeley is going it alone for now. She's building Startup Studios, a company that creates video courses to help startup companies and entrepreneurs start and grow their business. Since her background is already in video, she's well-equipped to build a formidable product offering with her existing skills. She has everything she needs to get it running.

But that's relatively rare. It's much more likely you have one or maybe two particular skills, such as engineering, marketing, sales, design, or product management, and lack one or more of the others. You stand a much greater chance of success if you partner with other people.

That act of "Partnership with other people" can take a few different forms. The most common distinction is between co-founders, employees, or contractors. Let's look at each of these in turn.

Co-founders

The best option when you're getting started is to find a mix of co-founders that can do all the things you need to get to revenue.

Finding a suitable co-founder is a challenge. Renee equated starting a company together to being in a marriage, and I have heard that analogy from many others. Since I am intimately familiar with both, I can validate that it does indeed have similar characteristics.

Co-founding means that you are binding yourself to one or more other individuals in a very close way, that includes practical, emotional, and financial, and legal aspects.

It is practical because you are signing up to work long hours alongside this other person or persons for the next five or maybe ten years. You'll be in meetings and conversations many times a day, and will be working nights and weekends together more often than you probably want to admit to yourself right now.

It is emotionally taxing because business is emotional. Building products is hard. Selling is hard. Hiring and firing is hard. Raising money is hard. Building a new company will push your emotional resilience to the absolute limits. Things will be going wrong all the time, and you will be under extreme amounts of stress. It is in those moments when who you chose as your co-founders can either make or break the company.

And it is financial because you are agreeing to take on risk, and possible reward, with another person. You are entangling your financial futures, both the upside and the downside. That can be very sticky territory for some people.

It is legal because there is usually legally binding paperwork that you submit to the authorities. Should things go horribly wrong, there will likely be lawyers involved to disentangle everything.

Renee explored the co-founder route at first. She has a strong network of engineers and investors, and she had many meetings with potential co-founders. In the end, there just wasn't a great fit. She opted to move forward on her own rather than co-found a company with someone she wasn't absolutely sure about.

Shared Values

The first, and most important, factor in choosing a co-founder is your shared values. Regardless of whose idea it was, you and your co-founders are in it together. You all need to believe in the vision. You need to be sure that you share at least some fundamental values.

For instance, if you sell environmentally friendly kids products, you may not wish to pursue a partnership with Big Oil. You want to make sure that your co-founders feel the same way, so that if an opportunity to partner with Big Oil ever arises, you don't end up in a sour dispute over it. Or if your long-term goal is to build a privately held company that will last 100 years, you don't want co-founders that just want to "flip it" by getting acquired in 5 years.

Jonathan McCoy's latest startup adventure is OK Play, a company that makes tools for improving team performance and coordination. His co-founders are two long-time friends, one of whom, Darla, he's known for over 7 years. The other, Michael, worked with him for a few years at a previous company.

Darla and Jonathan had been talking about the startup mission for years. The pair would meet about once per month, along with a group of mutual friends, and would continue to refine the mission together. Eventually, Jonathan found a pragmatic approach for execution, the timing was just right, and Darla decided she was ready to jump into the new startup with him.

Michael joined a month later. Since the two had already worked together, building product day in and day out at a tactical level, Jonathan knew what they could accomplish by working together. Michael agreed to come on board as well. Now the trio are powering through the incubator program at 500 Startups.

It doesn't always go this well, even with co-founders you know. A founder recently shared with me a familiar story. He and a close coworker quit their jobs and started a company together. They were both very passionate about the idea, and had reasonably complementary skills. It seemed like a great fit at first.

But these two had very different ideas about the vision for the company, and about how the work should be done. They failed to set clear boundaries and responsibilities from the beginning. Over time, they just pulled farther and farther apart, even going so far as dividing the newly hired team into two separate fiefdoms, one team reporting to each founder. Eventually, things boiled over and one of them had to leave the company. They are still on good terms, but a lot of hurt feelings and lost time and money were the result.

Complimentary Skills

Next you want to make sure you and your co-founders can contribute different skills to your startup. This may seem obvious at first. I typically see founders with a business background seeking engineering co-founders, and vice versa.

But it is more common than you think to have three or four co-founders who are all marketing people with similar backgrounds. People often start companies with friends or colleagues that they have worked with before. So it's actually a high probability that you all worked in the same job. I wouldn't try to talk you out of starting a company together. But you would need to make sure that only one of you is running marketing. The others need to take on other responsibilities--even if that means learning totally new skills, like sales, or even coding.

Resolving Conflict

You will disagree with your co-founders about all sorts of things, large and small. Again, like marriage, it isn't healthy or helpful to try to avoid disagreements. What matters is how you resolve them.

Conflict resolution is a whole category of learning by itself, and there are many great books and resources out there. I can't really do it justice here in this format.

But I would simply suggest that you and your co-founders have some shared language and process in place in advance for how you plan to resolve disputes.

And here I don't mean legally. I mean, on an emotional level, you and your co-founders presumably like each other. And as with any persons you care about, just like a parent and child, or a significant other, you'll want to make sure you have the emotional maturity to hear each others' concerns, and to seek out compromises that work for all parties involved.

If you and your co-founders have already had trouble communicating your concerns, fears, hopes, and desires, and you then drop that shaky relationship into the pressure-cooker of building a startup together...

Well, let's just say it's not going to be good.

Hiring

Not everyone who is excited about working with you on your startup is going to be an ideal co-founder. Some will lack the experience or the conditioning. Others will just not be in a financial position to take the same level of risk you are.

But, you may still want to recruit them for your startup as an employee. Here are some things to consider when hiring your first team members.

Timing

Knowing exactly when to hire can be tricky. It's better to hire slowly and be sure it's the right hire at the right time. You'll feel pressure to hire, because there is always more to do than hands available. Don't succumb to the temptation to hire without doing the proper checks.

For starters, don't hire for abstract purposes, or because you think you may need a marketing person or an engineer soon. Instead, you should wait as long as possible before hiring. If you can't afford employees, don't hire them.

The fastest way to run out of money is hire too many people before you have the revenue flow to retain them. Only hire when you are able to pay regularly. More specifically, only hire when you are in a position where you are losing money by not hiring them.

Compensation

You must pay a fair market rate for your employees. You will hear other opinions on this, folks who suggest you can recruit staff that will take a pay cut for the joy and thrill of being in a startup. People will say equity can make up for some amount of lower compensation. People will say startup employees will work for less because they know the startup can't afford market rates.

Those people are wrong.

You illustrate two things by how you compensate your employees. First, paying a full market salary shows that you respect what people are worth for their labor. That will in turn earn their respect and loyalty. Second, you show that you have a viable enough business that you can afford to pay the people you hire what they are worth. Paying them less is basically admitting that your company is not mature enough yet to have employees.

Now, I am not saying you can or should compete with Google or Facebook on salary. What I am saying is that, as of this writing, the annual salary for a senior engineer in San Francisco is something like $150,000. If you try to hire a senior engineer for $80,000, that missing value has to come from somewhere, and it's usually the experience and quality of the engineer. In other words, you'll get exactly what you pay for. If you can't afford to hire a senior engineer for $150,000 (plus all the added costs), then you can't afford a senior engineer.

When you hire someone for a startup, make sure you are clear about the risks. Startups fail often, and some potential employees may not have had the experience of working in a startup environment. If that unfortunate day comes when you have to tell the team you're out of money, you want to have set their expectations way ahead of time.

A word on equity. Maybe you've read my bio already. I survived the first "dot com" boom and bust. One of the things I recall vividly from those days was a few friends who gained high levels of paper wealth for a time, only to see most of it evaporate during the market crashes of either March 2000 or almost certainly September 2001.

It would be tempting to say that we as an industry have learned from our past delusions. There is all too much evidence, however, that we haven't. Most equity is frankly worthless. Probably including yours right now.

Equity is an important tool in motivating employees to contribute that little extra that they may not have contributed were they only paid in cash. But we must leave it at that. You still need to ensure that cash compensation is at fair market-rate for the role and seniority of the employee. Equity is not a replacement for cash.

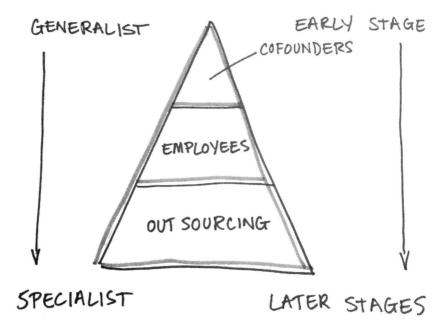

Figure 8. Progressing from early to later stages requires a different mix of people.

Outsourcing

There are times when it doesn't make sense to hire full time people. You may need a service that you can't do yourself. In those cases, it is common, and perfectly fine to hire outside temporary help.

Contractors and Freelancers

The most common form of outsourcing is freelance or contract work. The unwritten rule is that these services should not be your core value proposition, but rather some secondary aspect of your business.

Accounting is a great example. Most startups are not big enough yet to justify a CFO or a full time bookkeeper. Outsourcing your books to an accounting service is a reasonable expenditure. Branding, marketing, and copy-writing might also be good candidates.

Product development and sales are not.

I have come to believe that good sales requires that the seller firmly believe in the product. It is therefore very hard to outsource sales to someone who is not on the core team. It can be done, but only in later stages when you already have clear product-market fit.

Where founders also get into trouble is outsourcing the core product, as in the main value proposition, to a contractor or an agency. If you are building a technology company, you need a technology team on board. If you outsource the development of your product to a contractor, you are placing most of the risk of getting product-market-fit in the hands of someone whose incentives are to bill as many hours as they can. I would strongly recommend against this.

Agencies and Offshore Teams

I know agencies. I ran a web agency for nearly a decade, and worked as a senior employee for another several years later. And I have talked to many, many consultants over the years.

The agency model is always the same. They start out doing custom services for clients. But eventually, economic pressures enforce standardization. The only way agencies make money is to sell standardized services that they can deliver with increasing ratios of junior staff.

When you hire an agency, you are usually hiring the senior consultant in your mind. But you'll likely get shuffled off to the junior consultants sooner or later.

If you use an agency for anything, make sure it is a clearly delineated and encapsulated project, and not a core part of your value proposition.

Conclusion

The sections above are roughly in the order that you should deal with them as your startup grows. In the beginning, it is either just you, or you and your co-founders. Make sure you share values, have good communication practices, and the right balance of skills.

Once you are making some money, you can hire people to do work that you either cannot do or are too busy to do yourself. Don't hire until you can really afford it.

You can contract out non-essential services to freelancers and agencies. But remember that their economic incentives generally run counter to yours.

7. SOLVING THE RIGHT PROBLEM

Startups fail for many reasons. Most startups that fail in their first year or two, fail because they have not found a problem worth solving.

Sometimes the founders have the problem, but find that not enough other people have it. Sometimes they are seeing a problem where there isn't one. Or the problem isn't painful enough for customers to want to switch solutions. Or maybe the real painful problem is in some adjacent market segment.

To hit product market fit, you have to be solving a real problem for real customers. You need to confirm you have a real problem to solve. Then you need to confirm your solution is worth paying for, repeatedly.

You can sense early on that you are solving a real problem. As a human, you'll recognize positive feedback when you see it. Sometimes just telling the customer about your product makes them to pull out their credit card. Watching the delight on their face as they use your product signals that you are onto something. The feeling that you are solving a real problem is priceless. It's a significant part of why many of us become entrepreneurs in the first place. To solve problems for people!

Positive qualitative feedback can mask the economic realities of surviving as a startup. In what follows, we are going to rely on quantitative measures. You need data to know you're solving a real problem. You need data to optimize your product team's development speed. And you need data to improve the quality of your product so it is hard for competitors to catch up.

Testing the Problem

Start by conducting "problem interviews" with target customers. You

31

should do this if you are just getting started. But you should also do this if you have a product built already, and you haven't done problem interviews.

The two best resources on customer interviews are the book Talking to Humans and the Grasshopper Herder blog, referenced in the Bibliography. For now, I'll give you the basics.

The main rule of problem interviews is do not talk about your solution. I am not kidding. This isn't a sales meeting, and it's not a solution or usability test. This is a study to verify your target customer has the problem you think they do. You are there to listen and take notes.

Here are the steps:

1. Make a simple persona for your target customer.

There are about a bajillion articles on customer personas on the Internet. But my favorite is by Janice Fraser and nicely summarized by Tristan Kromer on the Grasshopper Herder blog. It is a simple 4-up, one-pager with a sketch, demographics, behaviors, and needs/goals.

Figure 9. Janice Fraser taught me this simple 2 x 2 format for personas.

2. Make a list of potential customer problems for your interview script.

Using the needs/goals section of the persona, derive 3 to 5 problem statements. It's best if these are worded as "I" statements from the customers' perspective. List them on a sheet of paper that you bring with you to the interviews. Next to each problem statement, write Yes/No, and a scale of 1 through 5.

3. Interview your target customers about their problems, one at a time.

Find 10 to 20 people like your persona and invite them to coffee. If possible, bring your friend/partner/assistant to take notes for you. That way you can focus on conducting the interview and on listening carefully.

After some initial pleasantries, ask them about each problem, one problem at at time. You want to know if they have the problem or not. If they do, circle the "Yes" next to the problem. You also want to know, if they do have the problem, how painful it is to them. Have them answer on a numeric scale, 1 for not a big deal, and 5 for extremely frustrating.

Before completing the interview, ask them if they have any other problems in this area you didn't ask about. This last bit can provide unexpectedly awesome product ideas. Leave some space on your script where you can fill these new problems in.

4. Interpret the results.

After a dozen or so of these interviews, you should start to see some clear trends. But wait until you have all 20 interviews done before drawing conclusions. If you're having trouble finding 20 people who are your target customer, your persona is probably wrong.

Interpret the results by adding up all of the severity scores for each problem statement. Use 0 for "No", of course. You should have each problem ranked on a scale of 0 to 80 (20 answers with a maximum score of 5 each). Sort them from lowest to highest in that order.

Any problem with a total score under 30 is a waste of time. Any problem over 75 should have your full attention. Anything between 30 and 50 is probably just a nice to have. Those can be good for solidifying competitive advantage once you have soundly solved the most painful problems, 50 to 80.

The data should tell you whether or not you are solving a real problem. If you already have a product, you have hopefully focused your product on the problem that is most painful for most of your customers. If not, it may be time to pivot.

Great! So you have discovered a problem that is actually worth solving. And your initial product is a solution that customers appreciate enough to pay for. You know this because you have already succeed in charging money for your product. Right?

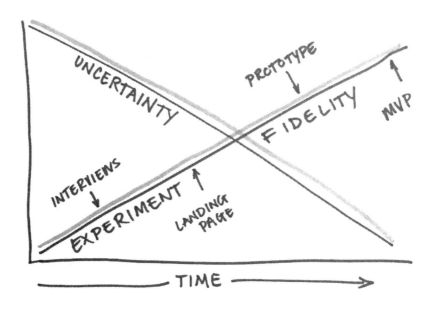

Figure 10. As we reduce uncertainty we earn the right to invest in higher fidelity tests.

Tip: Gradually increase the sophistication and fidelity of your experiments only as you reduce uncertainty in your product.

Testing the Solution

How do you know your solution solves the most painful problems effectively. Let's start by setting some target metrics that show we're on the right track.

Your average Customer Acquisition Cost (CAC) should be at about one third of your average customer's Lifetime Value (LTV). There is quite a lot of meaning packed into this deceptively simple statement. So, let's unpack it a bit.

There is plenty on the Internet (and in books, if you still read those) about CAC and LTV. So, I am not going to go into depth here. Bluntly, you will have to spend money on customer acquisition. It might be through advertising, content marketing, or direct sales. The cost of these activities, divided by the number of customers you get, will add up to your CAC.

Customers will pay for your solution. It may be a one-time sales transaction, or a recurring revenue model like a subscription. You want customers who buy once to return to buy from you again. This recurring activity is called Retention, which we discussed in the chapter on metrics.

Some will stop being your customers after a certain period of time, a concept called Churn. Churn is the inverse of retention. Perhaps you have solved their problem for good, or they no longer have the problem, or they (gasp!) found a better solution. In any case, the average amount of time they stick around is their customer lifetime. The amount of money they spent on your service or product during their lifetime is roughly their LTV.

Successful customer acquisition is more validation that you have identified a real problem. Retention of those customers is validation that your solution actually solves that problem.

To survive, you will need to acquire an increasing number of customers. And you will need those customers to buy more of your product or service, more often. Money earned through sales must be reinvested in building, delivering, and supporting the product. But it must also contribute to more customer acquisition.

Your revenue and retention should increase faster than your customer acquisition costs. Maybe your customer acquisition become more efficient as you learn to improve marketing. Maybe your revenue per customer increases because the product quality entices them to buy more or pay more per purchase. If you're not increasing LTV faster than CAC, your startup is in trouble.

Ideally, customers are converting on your site at an increasing rate. They are actively and enthusiastically using your product. And they promote it freely among their friends and coworkers.

So, let's say you are solving the right problem. Customer acquisition is not your only cost. You also have to develop the product, adding and improving capabilities, and quickly. After all, if you really have found a problem worth solving, it is quite likely others have too.

The competition is coming. You need to move faster, or they will eat your lunch.

8. BUILDING YOUR PRODUCT QUICKLY

In the last chapter, we talked about how to make sure your product is solving the right problem. It is time to talk about product development specifics. In this section, we're going to start tackling the nitty gritty of getting work done in a tech startup.

There isn't space in this short book to cover every kind of startup. To keep things simple, and because it's what I know best, I will focus on software products, specifically Software as a Service (SaaS). But even if you're building a hardware gadget, there are patterns and principles that you can apply from this section.

Defining the Work

The most important thing to get right is how you define the work that needs to be done. The past twenty-five years of software development has yielded some clear best practices. I will draw on those practices as a starting point, and extend our approach from there.

I am assuming you already have a good sense of your priorities because you have validated that you are, in fact, solving the right problem. We will come back to more finer-grained prioritization and decision-making below. For now, let's keep it simple.

This is not a book about Agile development, per se. There are already plenty of those, some of which I reference in the bibliography. But it's important we all get on the same page with basics before proceeding into advanced topics.

In Agile, we refer to a unit of work as a **user story**. For the rest of the chapter I will simply use the term "stories" to refer to these work items. A well-defined story starts with the user (or customer). It defines a specific goal the user is trying to accomplish with your software. The story is done when a user can realize some form of value by using the feature we are building. In other words, "done" means it is working properly and deployed to a place online the user can access. A feature isn't done until people are using it.

Stories work best when they are kept simple. They consist of a simple title sentence that summarizes goal for the user. They include visual assets that allow developers to understand the context of the story. And they include a set of testable criteria that ensure the story works as it should.

It is easy to go into too much detail writing user stories. This is especially true for product developers coming from an enterprise software background. Try not to get carried away with specifying requirements in exhaustive detail. Counter-intuitive as it may sound, it only leads to problems down the line. We'll explore some of those problems later.

Tip: Don't make user stories too detailed. Rely instead on frequent communication with the team.

For now, though, let's define our stories as follows:

"As a <user-type>, I want to <take-some-action>, so that I can <meet-some-need>."

We specify what type of user will be consuming this feature, what their goals are, and how we will know when that goal has been satisfied. A poorly written story is likely to create more confusion than it is worth. So, if you're going to write stories at all, make sure they are simple, clear, and concise.

Next, the assets attached to the story should be as lightweight as possible. We do not need high-fidelity visual mock-ups for each and every story.

Again, it is tempting to go overboard with the detail here. Don't just give your developer a high-fidelity mock-up and call it a user story. Mock-ups lie, both by misinformation and by omission. A hi-fi mock includes a large number of subtle and misleading assumptions. Unless a developer is very experienced, they may not push back on the assumptions depicted in the mock when they really should.

Thus, design mockups are imbued with an implicit authority they do not deserve. They imply that the design process is finished, when it rarely is.

And they discourage conversation because the mocks look so final. Plus, because they are just a snapshot, they leave out important details about the behavior of elements on the screen.

Instead, use mock-ups only for depicting and discussing new ideas. Consider them temporary and disposable as actual work artifacts.

A style guide or design framework enables designers to provide quick hand-drawn sketches. This greatly improves communication and clarity on the team. Maybe black and white digital wire-frames are in order periodically. But keep the visuals as lightweight as possible. Use frequent conversation between design and engineering to adjust the details of the story as you build it. We'll talk more about cross-functional teams below.

Tip: Avoid hi-fidelity mocks if possible. Use a design framework with quick sketches instead.

Lastly, a story should include a set of criteria that defines how we will know when it's working. These can be things like data that should be modified after the user takes an action. Or a minimal set of components that must be present on a screen. Or an alert or email message that is sent to the user afterwards. Whatever these criteria are, they should be the testable with automation wherever possible.

Stories with a simple title, concise criteria, and basic visuals allow developers to build them quickly. Thus they reduce the likelihood of miscommunication and rework.

Experiments

The Lean Startup movement has enhanced our understanding of User Stories with product experiments. Agile user stories were originally specified by a product owner who (theoretically) had a feel for what the user wanted. In the case of startups that clarity is rarely the situation. Instead, startup product teams should be using experiments to learn what users want from the product as they build it. We discussed the value of experiments from a business perspective in previous chapters. Let's look at how we incorporate them into our stories.

An experiment in product, just as in science, should start with a well-formulated hypothesis. A hypothesis is a proposed statement about the world that we want to validate or invalidate by collecting data. For example, the following is a trivial but well-formed hypothesis. "We believe that making the 'Buy Now' button red will result in higher conversion rates. We will know this is true if conversion rates increase by 10% in a sample size of 1,000 or more conversions."

I don't want to get bogged down in the details of this example. There is plenty of resource material on experiments out there for you to read on your own. I just want you to think about your product definition in the form of hypotheses, and how that might affect the structure of your stories.

Tip: Include your hypotheses on your stories as a separate section after the title, visuals, and feature criteria.

Epics

Before moving on with our stories, let's talk about epics. Some of your product ideas and experiments will be single stories, while others will be big concepts that must be made of lots of stories. These big concepts are often called epics. Think of them as containers for a set of stories that all go together. They will all be released to your users at the same time.

It's best to document your epics in a separate place from your stories (more on that in the next section). Then you can have your stories link or refer to the epics of which they are a part. It's possible, in fact, that your product experiments will be at the epic level, rather than the story level. That is perfectly fine.

Visualize the Work

You have defined the work as user stories. Next, you need to track what work is not yet started, what work is in progress, and what work is finished. You likely also need to follow whom on your team is working on what, whether that is together or separately. You do this by having some kind of visual control system for storing and displaying the work.

Why is this so important? Because work items in product development are physically invisible (see Reinertsen 2009). That makes it hard to see how much work you actually have, and where it is piling up. It's equally hard to tell who on your team is overloaded, and who is underutilized. And, most importantly, it's hard to see where high-priority tasks get stuck in your workflow.

By analogy, imagine you are in manufacturing. You can see all your raw inputs as they arrive at the factory. You have to track that material as inventory through the whole production process. In fact, you don't get to declare it as profit until after it has been assembled and sold as a finished product. Until then, you are carrying it on your books as a cost.

As material works its way from one work station to another, you can see the piles of partially assembled product between stations. If there is a blockage in the flow of work, it becomes immediately obvious. You can change the process on the factory floor to optimize the flow around bottlenecks. Or you can add resources to increase flow through a particular bottleneck.

For software development, you have to be able to see all the work, and track where work is stuck in your process at any given time.

There are many ways to visualize the work. You can use a simple to-do list in a notebook or a complex task management software such as JIRA. A to-do list is probably too simple for our purposes. It is important that everyone see each other's work, not just their own, and a to-do list will make that tricky. A tool like JIRA, on the other hand, is too complicated for a startup because you can get lost in all the features and configurations available to you.

My recommendation for startups is to start with a manual, physical system first. A whiteboard on the wall where the team works is usually ideal. If you must use a virtual system because some team members are remote, use the simplest system that will work.

Tip: Display your workflow on a board where everyone can see. Track the work as it flows through the process, not the tasks of individuals.

Kanban Systems

What I am describing is basically a Kanban system. The Kanban method (see Anderson 2010) teaches us the properties of a good visual control system. Here is how you get started.

First, diagram the current workflow from left to right as a series of columns on a board that the whole team can see (digital or physical). A column represents the "state" a work item is in, such as "Design" or "Testing". The first column is usually something like "Ideas", "Backlog", or "To Do". The last column is something like "Deployed", "Validated", or "Done". You can have as many columns as you have in your workflow.

Second, use sticky notes (on a physical board) to represent the work items. Keep work items on the board at the same level of scale. In other words, don't mix epics and stories. Use a separate board to track epics, and maybe even another for experiments.

Tip: Don't mix epics and stories on the same Kanban board. Use two different boards.

Third, and this is really critical, track the date on each story when a work item first enters the board. Update it whenever it moves between columns, and when it lands in the completion column. This allows you to calculate your team's cycle time. Cycle time is the elapsed time between when an item was started and when it was finished. This is your metric for everything else discussed in this chapter. You must use cycle time to measure improvement in the overall speed of your team.

Tip: If you don't measure cycle time, you cannot see if your team is improving.

Remember, one of the key benefit of visualizing your team's work is the ability to see where work is getting stuck in your process. For teams new to Agile or Kanban, there comes a surprising discovery. It is that the overwhelming majority of cycle time is accrued while work is waiting between steps.

These piles of work between steps are called queues. Queues are deadly to your business. Queues represent a ticking clock where partially completed work sits idle. You have invested time and energy in this work and it is just rotting away, unable to realize any value for you or the customer. It's unsold inventory, unused capacity, perishable goods sitting in a warehouse going rancid. You need to find and eliminate the queues in your process. This is the single most important thing that is keeping your team from going really, really fast.

The best way to reduce queues in a system is by constraining the batch size (see Reinertsen 2009). A batch is the group of items that are handed from one team member to another between work steps. The larger the batch size, the more likely there will be miscommunication, rework, and lower quality output.

Let's explore this with an example.

The team comes up with an epic for a new and exciting capability in the product. The theory is that this will attract a slew of new customers. In planning, the team breaks the epic into 12 stories.

The first part of the workflow for this team is design. The designer does the design specs for all dozen stories at once. They then hands them off to a developer to implement. That is a batch size of 12. This is a bad idea for several reasons. For one thing, the developer starts working on implementing the first story in code, while 11 stories sit accruing idle time. The designer can continue designing other features, but it's pointless. The developer already has a queue 11 items deep sitting there. Any additional work the designer does is just adding to the developer's queue, not moving things any faster through it.

But there is more than just time lost in a queue. Large batches also lengthen the feedback loop required for maintaining quality. Say there is an erroneous assumption in the design of the first story. The developer doesn't see it until all dozen are handed over together. Only then is the developer able to point it out to the designer, who must now go and rework all 12 designs. The designer just duplicated an error in 11 more stories for no good reason.

The best way to reduce the batch size in a workflow is use Work In Process (WIP) limits (see Anderson 2010). A WIP limit is an agreement to limit the number of items being worked on a time. It is implemented by putting a number at the top of one of the columns on the Kanban board. This number is an explicit agreement by the team that this column is only ever allowed to hold up to that number of work items. It is an acknowledgement of the importance of small batch sizes.

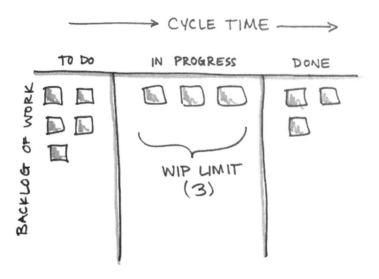

Figure 11. A Kanban board keeps all work visible all the time.

For all this to work smoothly, one last rule is needed. Work can only be pulled by a team member from a left column, never pushed downstream to the right. Pushing would quickly violate our WIP limits, and it only increases our batch sizes. A team member who is free for new work can take something from the top of the column to the left and start working on it. They do not take anything else until they have finished that work item. The effect of this is a smooth continuous flow of work.

So, we have constructed a Kanban system for our team. Great!

There is something else happening here that is worth pointing out. We are beginning to enable a self-organizing team. We did so implicitly, rather than declaring it. And we did it simply by constructing a process that enables self-organization. Because our system is so clear and easy to use, there is very little need for external direction from managers. We'll revisit this later, but I wanted to point it out here in this section where it first emerges.

Cross-Functional Teams

One way to reduce batch sizes is to build products as a cross-functional team. This is where your design, product, and engineering roles are working on the same small number of stories together. They can pair-program or just sit together at the same table. As long as the WIP limit applies to the whole team, and not individuals, you will end up with small batches.

Cross-functional teams create better products than teams organized into functional silos. The feedback loops are tighter, and so there is less rework and fewer miscommunications.

Trust me: Functional silos creep up on an organization, forming much earlier than we typically expect. I have seen startups as small as 5 or 6 people form functional silos. Business/product, design, and engineering tend to organically separate themselves by function. You have to work hard to counterbalance this tendency.

Tip: Have your product, design, and engineering folks sit together, and work on the same small number of stories together.

Optimizing for Space and Time

This brings us to the concept of trade-offs between space and time.

The ideal scenario situates everyone on the team together in the same physical workspace. Colocation is better for most startups than remote, distributed teams. Like cross-functional teams, proximity allows for a number of convenient optimizations. Many of these that we take for granted.

For one thing, the feedback loops are extremely tight. If the designer and developer are in the same room, a question about a design can be answered in a matter of minutes with a conversation. Sitting in different cities, that same conversation can be delayed hours or days. Video conferencing and chat programs (which I use exhaustively) cannot completely substitute for face-time.

A more subtle effect is also in play. Teams that work in the same physical place develop informal social bonds. These bonds are frequently undervalued by management and organization science. They form at lunch breaks or after hours. And they are extremely helpful in smoothing communication and resolving conflict.

You may think that five minutes huddled around a coworker's screen to look at a stupid YouTube video has little to do with building product teams. But you would be wrong. You would miss the crucial fact that teams work best when there is trust. And that trust forms as much informally and socially as it does professionally in work contexts. Ignore this phenomenon at your peril.

Tip: Colocate your cross-functional product team wherever possible. If you are distributed, make time to get together in-person frequently.

Finally, a word about cost-conscious remote hiring. If you are based in an expensive metropolitan area where technical talent is priced dear, using remote teams will seem tempting. However, for all the reasons above, the hidden costs of remote work dwarf any slight gains from lower labor costs.

If you have to use team members that are far afield from one another, apply Conway's Law.

Conway's Law states: Organizations that create information systems tend to produce architectures that mirror the communication patterns of the organization.

Wow, that's a mouthful! But think about it in terms of big companies. Teams produce components locally. Coordination between different teams tends to match the access patterns between the components themselves. This is a powerful idea!

Put another way, if you have to assign work remotely, assign a well-specified separate component. Make sure the component has a clearly understood interface to the rest of your system. Do not attempt to assign work remotely that is part of a cross-functional team. You will only be sad in the end.

Tip: If you must use remote teams, respect Conway's Law.

We have talked a lot about space. Let's talk a bit about time.

Your workflow is now visualized on a board that everyone can see. If there are bottlenecks forming in your system, they become apparent immediately. Team members can swarm around an issue and resolve it quickly. This will improve your cycle time overall.

How often do you need to check in as a team? I recommend daily, weekly, and monthly or quarterly cadences.

Cross-functional, colocated teams should always have a daily stand-up meeting. The daily meeting is used to coordinate the basic workflow. They should also have a weekly planning meeting to review progress toward major epics or to review recent experiments. And they should have a monthly or quarterly business meeting for longer term goals.

A Different Kind of Daily Stand-up

The purpose of the daily stand-up meeting is to make sure everyone has what they need to get their work done for the day. If you have been in stand-ups before, you may have experienced a pattern. Each person in turn states what they did yesterday, what they'll do today, and if they need help.

I want you to do your stand-ups differently.

Instead, huddle the team around the visual control board. Make the conversation about the work items on the board. Team members can still report if they need help. But the focus should be on moving items through to completion.

Why does this matter? Because utilization of individual team members is less important than throughput of the team overall.

Let me repeat that in plain English: Focusing on the productivity or utilization of your *individual* team members is a waste of your time. You have been taught that for your team to be efficient, everyone should be really busy all the time. That is wrong.

Your team is a complex system that includes cross-functional coordination. When everyone is loaded at or near full capacity, the system tends to build up queues. And when that happens, those queues can bring your throughput to a screeching halt. You have to keep some slack in your system in order to enable a smooth flow of work.

As such, it is far more important to focus on the flow of work than on the busy-ness of individual workers.

Tip: If everyone is busy all the time, queues will form in your system. If everyone is busy, these queues are extremely hard to dislodge.

Pulling it Together

Here is where we are so far. We learned how to define our work as user stories, including epics and experiments. We discussed how to design a work visualization system to track those stories through your workflow. We talked about the importance of colocated, cross-functional product teams. And we talked about cadences for planning and problem-solving the work. Do all these things, and you should be able to measure a dramatic improvement in your team's throughput in a matter of weeks. Next, we'll discuss the patterns of high-performing teams.

9. CULTIVATING HIGH-PERFORMING TEAMS

Exploring Teamwork

To explore the role of team building in a startup, we will look at two very different company cultures. One, GitHub, is a legendary tech startup known for their unique remote and non-hierarchical structure. The other, Sharethrough, is a shining example of Lean Startup methods carefully balanced with engineering excellence. The contrast should make the patterns stand out in sharper resolution.

...

Sonya Green's resume sort of jumps out of the pile. The eclectic mix of experiences in her background includes farming, house building, and bike repair, and topped with a Masters degree in Library Science. In short, she was not like any typical GitHub employee. After surviving a simulated support request they amusingly call "Kobayashi Maru" (named after a fictional training exercise from Star Trek), she was offered a part-time role in Customer Support. Three and a half years later, Green left her role at GitHub. Her title was Head of Web Support. From her vantage point, she had seen from the inside a legendary company culture that many in the tech scene aspire to replicate.

I met Rob Fan, CTO and cofounder of Sharethrough, at a mixer at the Lean Startup Conference in 2012. We have been talking shop ever since. Rob Slifka is VP of Engineering at Sharethrough. The two Robs (known around the office by their last names) are both influential voices on engineering leadership.

Both Robs, and Green, were part of a recent conference on engineering leadership that was held here in SF this fall called "Calibrate". I had the pleasure of attending this event. After watching their talks, I just had to get their input for this topic.

Hiring Generalists versus Specialists

Hiring is one of the most important things you will do as a company. After all, you are not just building a product. You are building an organization that is intended to survive for a long time. Hopefully, it will produce many new and innovative products during its lifetime.

Since it is people that make an organization, it is no small matter which people you bring in and when.

One of the first aspects to consider is whether to hire individuals with specific skills or those with more general experience. You will likely need a mix of both, and the mix will change over time.

Generalists are most valuable at the beginning of a startup. You haven't necessarily found product market fit yet. It is advantageous to have a small number of people with a broad range of skills. As you develop a core competency providing a specific product or service for a specific market, and as your systems get more complicated, specialization becomes a virtue.

Specialization should emerge out of a specific business need, says Fan. The first version of your product might leverage an external service, but you later decide to rebuild it internally. There has to be a strong business case for doing this. The component must be a core part of your business. But once that decision is made, the team that builds it will almost certainly become specialists in that area.

This can be challenging because engineers tend to want to generalize by default. They are engineers because they are curious about how things work, and want to take everything apart and learn about it. Yet, it can be problematic when you're racing to bring a new product to market.

"The problem," says Slifka, "is that everyone wants to work on everything. But you can't have people learning new technology all the time. Of course, learning is critical. But to be efficient, you have to focus on a core set of skills or technologies, at least within a particular team." And, as Slifka points out, while people say they want to try new technologies, they can sometimes get stuck and frustrated switching contexts too often.

So, the challenges around specialization and generalization are real, particularly in engineering. Engineers who lack challenge are likely to leave your organization. You need to enable and empower them to develop their skills and knowledge, to be sure. But allow everyone to switch focus whenever they please, and you're unlikely to get anything done. Somehow, you need to strike a balance.

Specializations can also form organically, according to Green. At first, a team member may dabble in an area of the product that is new or interesting to them. They see a need because they themselves also use the product. If they receive positive feedback for their efforts, they elevate themselves as a domain expert in this particular area. Requests for fixes in that area may then be routed to them in the future.

This creates a positive feedback cycle. People focus on those areas of the system where they are most knowledgeable and most effective. Gradually, specialization emerges.

As organizations grow, it becomes harder to be a generalist, and a focus in a few specific areas can help team members develop. There is a mythology that in the beginning GitHub engineers worked on what they want to. The reality is more nuanced. In theory, a strong culture can compensate for what would otherwise be chaos. The ideal wasn't true for everyone, and maintenance wasn't a focus. In some ways it worked, and in some ways it didn't. Green has reservations about the universal effectiveness of the model, without adequate organizational and cultural structure. Certainly growth has pushed GitHub toward more structure over time. Who knows how that will affect their culture in the long term?

Regardless, the GitHub model won't work everywhere. For Fan and Slifka, allowing engineers to work on whatever they want can distract from the strategic direction of a business, unless your business is one where the engineers have an acute understanding of the core need. Indeed, Green points out that as GitHub has grown into a more robust enterprise-grade solution, the free-for-all approach had started to break down.

Generalization seems to be most critical at early on. Specializations emerge from specific pain points. Your specific needs should drive whether you identify and tackle those pain points by explicit strategy or ad-hoc self-assignment.

Process: Cross-functional Teams and T-Shaped People

We have discussed specialization and generalization by looking at the individual. But your process must also balance these forces.

Process tends to be a dirty word in the "moving fast and breaking things" zeitgeist of Silicon Valley. But, rest assured, teams that do not define and document their process early almost certainly fail.

In a cross-functional team, it is useful if people are T-shaped. By T-shaped people, we mean people who are deep in one area, but broad in many others. This is particularly useful when those people work in a linear workflow. If a person specializes in one step in the workflow, we want them to be familiar with the adjacent steps.

For example, suppose your workflow involves distinct phases such as design, development, and testing. It is useful for a designer to know a little development, and an engineer to know a little design. The hand-offs between them will require fewer back-and-forth communications. There will be less re-work.

Cross functional teams often rally around a specific business theme or goal. The team includes all functions necessary to build features in that theme. Their process is less likely to be linear, and more of an ad-hoc collaboration.

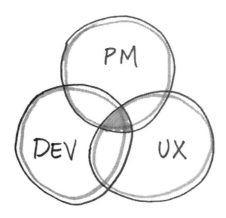

CROSS-FUNCTIONAL TEAMS

PM

DEV   UX

OF T-SHAPED PEOPLE

Figure 12. Good product teams are co-located, dedicated, and cross-functional.

"All our teams are cross-functional," adds Slifka, "and that enables them to be quite autonomous in how they get their work done." Slifka explains that the teams have everything they need to carry a new feature from concept to deployed functionality.

There is a relationship, he explains, between autonomy and efficiency. You can be more efficient if there is a high degree of consistency and heterogeneity in the work a team is doing. Once you have to move people around, you start incurring costs of context switching and domain ramp-up.

At GitHub, in the beginning, when there was less of a notion of separate "teams", everyone was more T-shaped than not. Again, specialization was based partly on personal interests and ability. Empathy is critical in groups with such a loose formal structure, says Green. At GitHub, decisions must be made by those with domain knowledge enough to make the right call. For such a process to work, there needs to be a high degree of trust. Trust can only develop over time by way of feedback loops and frequent and high-quality communication.

Remote/Distributed versus Co-located Teams

Speaking of communication, are we talking about face-time or video chat? Email or meetings? That depends on whether your team is a distributed team or located in the same physical space. Here, GitHub and ShareThrough sharply diverge.

GitHub was built using GitHub, says Green. It is a special case that the product they were building was a process tool for engineers. That meant they could leverage its functionality to organize building the product itself. Few teams will find themselves in a similar situation.

The legendary structure at GitHub, with most employees working remotely, was made possible using GitHub as a process and a tool. There is an extremely open and transparent culture. A bias for having conversations in the open, where appropriate, reduces some of the communication friction that exists in other organizations.

Sharethrough is definitely not making something for use by engineers. The end-user of the product is a different persona than the teams building it. As such, Sharethrough is more like most other companies.

It can makes sense to have a remote team is when you have a specific, time-boxed project that is tightly scoped. This requires a high degree of specification, which means you need to know exactly what you're building and how to build it. There is little room for creativity.

Physical distance increases the cost of communication. Paradoxically, it also increases the need for regular communication.

New and innovative projects are best handled by dedicated, co-located, and cross-functional teams. In creative and experimental work the transaction cost of feedback is high, the risk of miscommunication great. With remote teams, you can't afford to have too much back and forth, and yet that is precisely what innovation requires.

Green too acknowledges that chat technology isn't always the best communication means. Even in a distributed culture, there is a need for regular one-on-one time, in person or with video. These interactions help build trust, but that trust degrades asymptotically over time. You have to keep it going to preserve social bonds.

Roles and Boundaries

Roles at GitHub early on tended to be more informal and based on ability and interest. You build credibility by doing things right according to the observations of your peers. This method of assigning tasks can work only if the engineer herself is the end customer. Over time, growth and success have imposed a hierarchical structure on the one-time engineering utopia.

If that is not the case, solid product management is required, say Fan and Slifka. The internal structure of the team can be autonomous and fluid, but the boundaries between the team and the business must be clear.

A team responsible for a specific component can be as loose with role definition as they want, within the confines of that scope. But in their relationship to the rest of the business, or to other teams, they need to have a clearly defined domain of expertise.

Visibility and Predictability

In any business, you must have some idea of what you are building, for whom, and approximately when it will be ready for sale.

As we've noted, GitHub was solving a problem that every engineer had. Since engineers are the primary customer, the people building the product had strong empathy for the end user. Their rapid early success then made it possible for them to have low pressure on specific project timelines. As a result they developed a loose culture of authority around what gets done when. That dynamic has reportedly begun to change as the pressure of being an enterprise software company has increased.

You have to build capacity and trust over time before you can provide any reliable visibility to the business. These days, Fan doesn't spend his time dwelling on the inner workings of each team. But that's alright. In fact, it's essential. If he had to look over everyone's shoulder all the time, he laughs as he tells me, no-one would get anything done. Instead, layers of abstraction between teams regulate the scope of visibility and decision-making.

But how do you get there?

You start out in the beginning just trying to get your first product out the door. But eventually, says Fan, every startup needs a clear product roadmap aligned with the business strategy.

You can only develop predictability over time and that builds trust with the business. Start small at first, with shorter time horizons of maybe a couple weeks. Gradually, as the team is able to produce results reliably, the business learns to trust their estimates. You can then extend the planning horizon to months or even quarters. But you have to learn to walk before you can run.

The more complex the business model, or the more diverse the stakeholders, the more strategy and planning become necessary. Which of the above methods you use will depend on the business you are in, the subject matter, the revenue model, and many other variables.

10. DEALING WITH COMPETITION

Competition can be a great motivator, but it can also be a big distraction. As we build our startup, we must think about how our actions fit within a larger business ecosystem where other players are competing for market share.

Your Ideal Mindset

Competition is a good thing for startups. If you have competition, it means there is probably a viable business there somewhere, because other organizations are already trying to service it.

Don't let the existence of competitors psyche you out. But don't bend your whole strategy around what others are doing either.

There are two scenarios I have seen over and over in my time as a technology consultant. They represent the two extremes on a continuum of strategies and approaches for thinking about and dealing with your competition.

Try to imagine these two hypothetical startup founders:

First, you have a founder who has worked for a decade or more in a firmly established industry, and is now leaving the safety and security of employment because they believe they have identified a pain point that their former employer is ignoring. They set out to do their first startup as a direct reaction to their frustrations with the firmly entrenched incumbent.

And maybe it is a really good idea. Maybe their new idea solves a real, painful problem in the market. Better still, this founder knows the customers really well, because they recently were one. And they have spent the last decade networking with peers just like themselves, so they probably have a big contact list of potential customers.

But this founder is carrying a massive amount of confirmation bias, and must overcome it by carefully validating the problem with others. By having worked inside the industry for so long, they carry with them innumerable subtle biases about the market and about customers, biases that developed over years of working for an incumbent on the inside.

As a result, the founder's mindset is far on the side of thinking too much about the competition, and one big competitor in particular. They are likely to frame most of their thinking relatively, in reaction to what they experienced working for the big guy.

Second, you have a founder who is relatively new to their market. Perhaps they have startup experience, either working in startups for others, or even having founded one or two themselves, successfully exiting or not. In short, they have the requisite startup experience to make this work in general.

But what is distinct is that this idea is in a market that is entirely new to them. They believe they have identified a problem from afar that they can solve. Maybe it's a mass consumer issue they experience themselves. Perhaps personal organization or delivery services. Or maybe music and file organization, on-demand fashion advice, medication reminders and other "quantified-self" apps.

Or maybe it is just born from an observation of some way that technology could assist a market segment they interact with regularly as a customer, but have never worked in. I think of scheduling apps for small businesses, or point-of-sale systems, or various logistics solutions. The founder thinks they understand the customer and the problem, but it is highly unlikely they know much about the competitive landscape.

These are the two extremes. One pays way too much attention to the single 800-pound gorilla competitor (maybe their former employer). The other pays very little attention to competition because they are so enamored with their new idea, they blissfully and ignorantly wander into a crowded bloodbath of a competitive landscape.

My overall advice, and I will break it down below, is to not be either of these two extremes. Balance between them, learning everything you can about the competition but not getting obsessed with any one competitor.

You have to stick to your vision. And if your vision is completely encapsulated by the business operations of some competitor, it is probably not big enough.

Understanding The Market

In nearly all cases, assuming you have identified a real problem, and are prepared to bring a technology solution to market quickly to address that problem, you will be competing for your customer's attention with other firms trying to solve the same problem.

Venture capitalist, Mark Suster, has argued for taking the time to really understand the market before you get too far ahead of yourself. Understanding the market means several things.

You should know the approximate size of the market. How much money are people or organizations spending each year to solve the problem you are solving with your product? Be a good researcher and verify this with more than one source. If you are going to need venture capital, you had better know the answer to this question, and be able to back it up with data.

How is the market structured? Is it highly fragmented with lots of players, or is it mostly dominated by one large player? If there are many, how are you going to cut through the noise and differentiate yourself? If it's one, how are you going to unseat that mammoth organization from dominance?

Think also about growth and change in the market. Is it saturated and stagnant, or is it constantly growing and changing? How long has the market existed? Is this cloud computing and data science or shipping and logistics? Is it virtual reality or task management? It makes a huge difference whether the market is old or young, in terms of how many competitors there are, and how easy it is for them to rise or fall.

A Defendable Competitive Advantage

You'll have to differentiate yourself no matter what the market looks like. Your problem interviews and other research can tell you how customers solve their problem now, what solutions they currently use. Make sure you identify not only what is different about your solution or approach, but what's unique about your capabilities that would be difficult for a competitor to replicate. If you focus your message on differentiation that is easy to copy, you'll have to keep changing your message when competition catches up. That will erode customers' confidence.

Even more importantly, you should only compete on feature areas that are in alignment with your product strategy. Just being different isn't enough. Your product and product lines should evolve over time as you move your company toward your vision.

If you see an opportunity for differentiation that is attainable given your current state and capacity, but represents a clear departure or sidetrack from your strategy, consider it very carefully. Maybe you need to pursue it this time for financial reasons. But that is a slippery slope. I have seen too many companies (including one of my own) become scattered and confused because of a lack of focus brought on by pursuing a "just for right now" opportunity.

Not every competitor will be a competitor forever. As business models shift you may find yourself in competition with a former partner. Or you may find a partnership opportunity with a competitor. Make sure you think carefully about how you might turn competition into a symbiotic relationship. Maybe it's services vs product. Maybe it's bundling. Maybe it's apps versus a platform. There may be ways where your capabilities fit nicely with gaps that they currently have. This isn't war. We are all trying to make money here, and yesterday's enemy can be tomorrow's ally.

Map It Out

You'll want to visualize all of your competitors on some kind of model. So, let's talk through some options now.

I recommend using a simple 2 x 2 matrix. There's an inside joke that consultants are always suggesting everything fit into such a matrix. But in this case, I think it's actually helpful!

The benefit of a matrix depends on what your axes represent. You'll want to identify two very important dimensions that your competitors fall into, and use those for the x and y axes of your matrix.

For example, maybe in your market there are companies that serve mostly small businesses and others that serve mostly enterprise. Maybe there are more manually configurable solutions and more automated solutions. You'll need to find the two most important axes in your field (and there is no right answer here). You'll then plot all of your competitors on this Cartesian plane–including yourself.

What this can tell you is two main things.

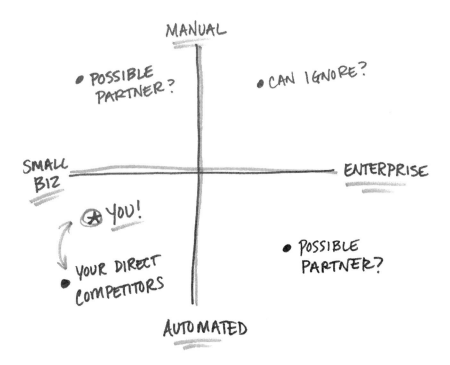

Figure 13. Plot competitors on a matrix to expose potential partners and direct threats.

First, the competitors that end up in your quadrant on the matrix are probably most similar to your company (at least according to those two dimensions you picked for x and y). You will want to make sure that your differentiators from them comprise skills, assets, or capabilities that are very hard for them to reproduce. Maybe it's your data, your team, your exclusive access to some resource or channel. Whatever it is, you need to be able to defend it fiercely.

Second, the competitors that end up in the quadrants adjacent or diagonal from you might in fact be opportunities for partnership. Say they serve enterprises while you serve SMBs, and they have a custom solution while yours is highly automated. Could there be a reason to partner with them either for bundling or wider distribution? Maybe it's worth reaching out to see what they think.

Conclusion

Remember, there is nothing inherently bad about having competition. If there isn't any you should be worried.

Keep your vision always front of mind when thinking about how you compete. Avoid the trap of copying what others are doing.

Identify your unique defendable advantages. Identify complimentary advantage where you can partner as well.

With the right mindset, and clear vision, companies can and do compete very successfully. That mindset is strongly influenced by your organizational structure and company culture. That's the topic of our last two chapters.

But first, let's look at raising capital.

11. RAISING MONEY: HOW TO GET YOUR STARTUP FUNDED

The venture capital aspect of building startups is heavily overemphasized here in the Bay Area. At least compared to minor things like, oh, I don't know... product development or fostering good company culture!

But funding has a role to play in company-building, and it is important that you understand whether, when, and how you might need it. It's going to come up one way or another if you're building a startup company, and you are going to have to deal with it. Even if that means deciding not to raise money, you still need to understand what you're deciding exactly.

To be honest, I have never raised money for a startup myself. At least, not as the founder, the one whose neck is on the line. Oh, certainly, I have been the technical guy in the room before. I have done the "ride-along" thing on many investor pitches, I know a lot of investors personally, and have talked to them a lot. And I have been to way more "demo days" and "pitch contests" than I would care to admit.

So while I have not personally experienced the emotional rollercoaster of raising money, I have seen it up close. And nearly every founder interviewed for this book has raised funds. I've already received a lot of input on it from these amazing entrepreneurs.

Still, to cover this topic well, I wanted to get some expert opinions on the matter, straight from the source. I reached out to a couple friends from the investment side, to get their take on what you need to know as you navigate the treacherous waters of startup funding.

I first met Angela Tran Kingyens from Version One when I was researching methods to quantify early stage startup risks using Monte Carlo simulations

(What?! Yeah, I know. Check the website for this book to read my article on that). Despite all the talk about using data to drive investment decisions, it was incredibly hard to find anyone actually using advanced financial methods to evaluate risk in startups.

Version One is a thesis-driven, values-driven, and data-driven investor. They focus on the true early stage, from pre-Seed to Series A funding rounds. Before becoming a VC, Angela cofounded a YC-backed education company that helped academics transition into careers in data science. She knows what it is like to be an entrepreneur, which I was surprised to learn is not all that common among investors.

Investors Are People

If you are going to raise money, you're going to be having a lot of meetings with investors. You'll be better off in those meetings if you can build a little empathy for where they're coming from. So, let's try to understand investors a bit.

Imagine you're just sitting down for coffee with an investor for the first time. What's going on in her head?

The first thing to understand is that they meet a lot of people. Investment is a relationship business. A good amount of their time is spent simply having coffee with entrepreneurs, looking for the next deal. Lots and lots of coffees. They just came from a meeting before yours, and they have another one right after yours. Probably a good idea to keep that in mind.

Angela spends about two thirds of her time doing this. One-on-one meetings, events, dinners, and other networking events with entrepreneurs, operators, and other investors. It's the toughest part of the job to scale, and that's because of the relationship aspect. But this is where they get their deals from. It's absolutely critical for their business model.

Tawny Holguin also has hands-on startup experience. As a partner at the legendary Andreessen Horowitz, she focused on early stage investments. Before Andreessen Horowitz, she ran operations for the gifting startup, Wantful. She knows what life is like in the trenches of a fast-growing startup in the epicenter of innovation.

One of the surprising aspects of investing, says Tawny, is that it's so nuanced, so dependent on subtle human factors. Do you and the investor click? It's more of a personal aligning of values and interests than founders typically appreciate.

And you just can't know what biases the investor might have because of past experiences. Maybe they were burned before by a similar investment opportunity. Who knows? There just has to be a human connection there for the relationship to progress.

There is no way to automate this "getting to know you" process. Sure, there are data-driven approaches. But at the end of the day, you and the investor have to like each other. And you have to believe in each other.

That probably seems unfair to founders who, rightfully, wished to be evaluated on the merits of their idea, the skills of their team, their passion for the vision, or the metrics they have carefully assembled.

And yes, that stuff matters too. But the empathy piece really is the key.

After all, "it's not hard to be an average investor", says Angela. If you follow the trends, you'll very likely do OK. Somewhere in the middle of the curve.

But it's very hard to be an excellent investor.

What makes an excellent investor? You have to have empathy for founders, says Angela. You don't have to have experience as a founder, though it helps.

But the really great investors are those that connect with you on an emotional level. The really great investors have the people thing down. Without that, they might as well just do derivatives trading.

Great investors think out of the box even as they are thesis driven. They make bets on the fringe and go against the grain, and they don't follow consensus. It's frequently said that VCs are actually fairly conservative. These, then, are the average. The truly great ones take risks and invest ahead of the curve.

What Do They Look For?

Both Angela and Tawny emphasized the importance of passion for the space you're in and the problem you are trying to solve. Investors are somewhat less interested in the opportunistic founder, just doing a startup for its own sake.

You need to be able to tell a compelling story about why you are building your company. Ultimately, the investor is backing you, not just your idea. So be crystal clear about where you come from, and why you're doing this at all.

It's also important to do your homework. Make sure you're talking to the right investors. Angela's team, for example, invests in startups leveraging strong network effects, such as marketplaces. Some firms prefer investing only in technology innovation. Is your startup a technology innovation, or is it a business model innovation? Which investors are interested in your space, in your specific area of expertise. It pays to do your research and come prepared.

Tawny emphasized how important it is to really know everything about your industry. How big is the market? Who are the competitors? What are the trends? You have to be able to talk intelligently about the space you're operating in. You should know more than the investors about what's going on there. They expect that of you.

Understand VersionOne's thesis, says Angela. Pitch in a way that aligns with their values. In short, make sure you're talking to the right investor.

Again, it's that empathy piece. Are you bringing the investor something of value or just wasting their time?

Do your homework before scheduling any meetings.

When To Raise?

For starters, there is a hint given the placement of this chapter within the book. Specifically, it comes after the part on solving the right problem, building your MVP, and dealing with the competition.

You simply cannot raise money from investors these days without some amount of traction. Oh, sure! There are going to be exceptions to this. But not for you. The exceptions are for founders that have firmly established records of success.

If the investor places an emphasis on technology breakthroughs, says Tawny, you should probably have something significant to show, and something that illustrates your team's technical expertise.

If your startup is not innovating specifically on technology, but rather on the customer segment or business model, you should be talking to an investor that focuses on those kinds of companies.

Maybe not having a CTO in place is OK at this stage. But if your focus is a tech innovation, I've found that there are definitely firms that will be turned off by founders who have outsourced all of their technology development to a development shop.

Finally, Angela says investors bristle at funding pitches for the sake of founders paying themselves. The investment should be for growth, hiring, and so forth. If you haven't bootstrapped for a few months, and built something meaningful that has traction, you should probably not be scheduling pitches.

Get the witch's broom first. Then go see the Wizard. The Wizard's not going to pay you to figure out how to get the broom. That's your job.

Figure 14. There is no short-cut for the hard work of proving product-market fit.

12. FIRST, STOP CALLING US RESOURCES!

Attention is a curious thing. I had wanted that coffee so bad an hour ago, and yet I had let the second half get cold. I was so absorbed in coding, I didn't notice the time go by. I also didn't notice my coworker approach until she was practically standing right in front of me.

"You're not going to like this," she said. She stood, hugging her Macbook Air to her chest, weight shifted to one leg, like someone who'd been hiking for an hour and finally stopped at a crest to take a breather. I had barely glanced up yet, but I could already feel her searching for an initial reaction.

She was a product manager, and really good one. I enjoyed working with her immensely. In fact, I am the one who had recruited her into the company. I felt guilty for all of the nonsense she had to deal with now, as if I had sold her a defective bag of goods when I convinced her to join us. Unfortunately, as a product manager in this company, she didn't report to me. And so I had little direct control over what her day to day was actually like. Technically, I was a more senior member of the company. But due to way things were organized, she frequently had more access to important meetings than I did.

I closed my laptop and glanced up. The look on her face said it all.

"Oh, what now", I sighed? I didn't even try to project the glossy professionalism of an engineering director in a 200 person, high-profile tech startup. She knew me too well to be bothered by my informality. We had one of those unofficial comradeships that form in companies. It was the kind where you don't technically work together much, but your values are aligned and so you informally try to make change together. We were a tiny alliance, on our own crusade to bring some semblance of vision and strategy to this wayward company.

"Yet again…" She paused, as if tasting the words for accuracy before spitting them out. "Yet again, they have completely changed their minds about our priorities. He's going to come talk to you about shifting your resources again." As she said, "resources", the word was dripping with sarcasm.

Shifting resources. It really burned me that our CEO still always referred to human beings that worked in our company as resources. It was like a conceptual splinter that had lodged in his brain during his MBA, and he just completely lacked the tools to tease it out. Resources. Like barrels of oil, or watt hours of electricity. Not creative, sensitive, thinking beings.

She sighed deeply, plopping down in the oversized armchair next to me in the small, quiet sitting area where I was working. It was one of the few places in the cavernous loft in SOMA where I could actually get some work done. Someone, somewhere had decided that all startup engineering teams should work in open floor plans with high ceilings. You know, so that everyone can hear every murmured comment from every other pair of engineers in the room. The din drove me batty every day, and I regularly searched the office space for a quiet corner.

My colleague had just come from a meeting with the three other product managers and our CEO. No-one from Engineering had been invited. She'd mentioned the meeting on her way to it about 90 minutes ago. I was expecting bad news to come out of it, and yet naively holding out hope for good.

"So, how much has changed?" I took a tentative sniff of my cold coffee, thought better of it, and set it back down. Sometimes I drink beverages just as a nervous habit. That's probably why my caffeine intake is so high. I can't think without a warm mug within arm's reach. It's a habit I picked up early in my career, and I just can't shake it.

"Everything, basically. All the department heads got together last week at the executive offsite. Apparently, they horse traded the product and engineering teams around again. Everyone has their pet projects, as you know."

This was particularly painful. As Director of Engineering, I should in theory be allowed to organize my teams as I saw fit. However, our CEO saw things differently. He insisted on being involved in every "resource allocation" decision. As a result, my role was more of a coach than a manager. I was powerless to do much more than advocate. I didn't have absolute hiring, firing, or even assignment powers. And yet I was still responsible for 24 direct reports. I felt more like the Director of the Kanban board most days.

"Then why did we bother with that all-company offsite three months ago? We were supposedly setting the product strategy for the rest of the year." I said this rhetorically, knowing full well she couldn't provide a satisfying answer. "I certainly could have done without a weekend of ropes courses with 150 of you clowns. Sheesh!"

She smiled at my mock insults. "You probably should go talk to him. Try to get ahead of whatever's coming your way."

"Yep," I said. I picked up my laptop and started over to the CEO's office at the far corner of the loft, for what would likely be a very frustrating conversation.

"This'll be fun," I muttered to myself as I walked.

...

This story is mostly a work of fiction. It is a composite of different experiences I have had over the years, and stories I have been told by others. There are about a half dozen startup patterns related to culture that are woven into the narrative above, each of which we'll cover in the next chapter.

So what do we mean by "culture"? Culture is not something you can control directly. When I Google culture, I get this choice little snippet:

"A culture is a way of life of a group of people–the behaviors, beliefs, values, and symbols that they accept, generally without thinking about them, and that are passed along by communication and imitation from one generation to the next."

The keywords here for me are "values" and "beliefs", and the phrase "generally without thinking". For our purposes, those three pieces pretty much cover it.

We are going to establish the patterns that startups should strive for in building their cultures for success in the next and final chapter. However, here are some anti-patterns we can think about as a contrast for now.

Constantly shifting priorities.

If you have worked in technology for any amount of time, you have probably had product priorities switched on you from above, often without explanation. Little can demotivate a team faster than having them push toward a goal for weeks or months, only to have the goal changed without warning or explanation.

Who gets invited (and who doesn't) to which meetings.

Hate meetings? Yeah, who doesn't. But it's much worse to find out after the fact that you missed an important meeting because your participation was seen as unnecessary. Worse still when decisions that affect you or your team are made in your absence.

Who decides which teams work together.

Teams with clear goals and responsibility are ready and able to collaborate spontaneously. Undermining their autonomy only undermines their effectiveness.

The importance of space.

Knowledge work takes focus, and that is best done in private. Collaboration requires proximity with teammates and works well in open space. There is no perfect office space for all teams. Designing the ideal workspace takes time and money. But it pays for itself.

Product, design, and engineering working in silos.

That teams still have problems with silos in 2016 boggles my mind. And yet I hear all the time about this lack of cross functional integration.

Useless team building exercises in a strategy vacuum.

Off-sites are important for building camaraderie among team members. It can seriously backfire, however, if these social and team building exercises occur in the absence of a strong vision and clear strategy.

So if these are all anti-patterns, what should we do instead?

In the next chapter, we will lay down the foundation of what a good startup culture looks like.

13. PATTERNS OF GOOD STARTUP CULTURE

In the previous chapter, we pulled out some common organization and culture anti-patterns. But, of course, that begs the question:

What does a good startup culture look like?

Company culture has been in the news a lot lately. The term "culture" is used in different ways in the context of describing different problems in the firm or the organization. Here we mean it in a particular frame of reference.

This is a book about startups. Startups are temporary organizations in search of a scalable and repeatable business model (Blank, 2003). So we are concerned primarily with cultures that can enable that behavior.

Recall our borrowed definition from the last section:

"Culture is a way of life of a group of people–the behaviors, beliefs, values, and symbols that they accept, generally without thinking about them, and that are passed along by communication and imitation from one generation to the next."

A startup culture that produces behaviors, beliefs, and values that are required to make great products and scale business models typically have the following attributes:

- Experimentation is encouraged and rewarded.
- Feedback is frequent, honest, and always buy direction.
- There is both tacit and explicit agreement in the group on the vision of the company.
- Tasks are delegated with trust and without micromanagement.

I could probably list many more, but you get the idea.

A culture that encourages these behaviors can be designed intentionally. To do so, though, requires understanding some organizational and leadership patterns.

In what follows, I've tried to organize the positive patterns into themes for readability. But keep in mind that there is a lot of overlap between the themes.

Vision and Strategy

It all comes back to your vision. It's the vision that ties all the daily activities together. It should be ever-present in meetings, in correspondence, and even in casual conversations about company goals and strategy.

And not just the vision. The business strategy must also be apparent to everyone in the company. The strategy should be clear enough that anyone on the team can articulate it from memory, in their own words, to a stranger. If your strategy is too complicated to explain to a friend or an advisor who doesn't know the details of your business, then it's probably too complicated to work.

You can use your strategy to determine objectives for individuals or teams. The strategy should include each of the major capabilities you need to acquire or develop in order to achieve your company's goals. From the capabilities you can then derive activities you need to execute on in order to build that capability.

These activities from each capability can also be mapped to a series of measurable objectives. You can then use these objectives to measure the forward progress of people, teams, and the company as a whole. (For example, if you plan to use an OKR system, this process would be where your objectives come from.)

It is important that everyone understands the overall strategy and not just their or their team's own objectives. There will be times when objectives appear to be in conflict, or resources particularly scarce (or more than usual, let's say). The team leads will better be able to negotiate with each other, and have more empathy for each other's position, if they clearly see how they each fit into the strategy.

Leadership

What do I mean by leadership?

Leadership is the ability to inspire a group to operate collaboratively toward a common goal, separate and apart from any formal or official management or reporting structure.

That cuts both ways. Leaders can emerge with no formal hierarchy present. But it also means that while everyone may technically report to you as the founder or CEO, that does not guarantee that you can effectively lead them.

Certainly, you are expected to be a leader for your company. And as the company grows you will need to assemble a leadership team to help you build the company. Each member of this leadership team should be able to give you firm and direct feedback on your own leadership. You won't be a perfect leader, and you will need the observation and honesty of this group to get better at it. If they just tell you "yes" all the time, they are doing you a disservice. Seek out senior leaders who are unafraid to challenge you.

Your leadership team will look to you for signals of how to execute. You are their model. You must behave in a way that exemplifies how you want people in your company to behave. If you run around with your hair on fire all the time, jumping from one crisis to another, that will set the tone for the company. And in case you can't tell from my tone here: don't do that.

One of the biggest responsibilities of a leader is to train and cultivate other leaders. This is why, in his book "What to Ask the Person in the Mirror", Robert Kaplan emphasizes the critical importance of succession planning and effective delegation as key pillars of leadership.

When you hire someone who will report directly to you, that person is looking to you for guidance on how they can best fulfill the role. Kaplan recommends training them essentially to someday take your place. This is called "succession planning".

This mindset of training your replacement accomplishes several things at once:

It forces you to clarify exactly what it is that you do, so that you can explain it clearly to your team. Yes, they need to know what you do.

As you teach what you do, you must necessarily delegate some of your responsibility to your team. If you don't already delegate effectively, this will help you learn to do that.

71

You show your team how to train others once they are in the position of hiring their own team.

The entrepreneur leaders I have worked with have all struggled with delegation. The truly successful have found a way to let go of the sense that "I do everything here." That's a necessary step for scaling a company.

Decision Making

Another key aspect in company culture is establishing how decisions are made. There are literally hundreds of decisions to be made each week, some large and some small. You can't possibly be involved in all of them.

It's critical that you determine exactly which types of decisions you can delegate and which you must weigh in on. Too many companies are woefully unclear on this matter. Make sure your company isn't one of them.

There is a lot of science around decision making, and I won't go into too much detail here. In Flow: Principles of Lean Product Development, Don Reinertsen stresses the cost of decisions that must be escalated up the chain of command.

Instead of controlling every decision, he suggests creating decision rules that capture the economic logic of how you would want a decision to be made. Take care to set expectations ahead of time as to who is responsible for which decisions.

You should minimize those big, centralized decisions, if you can. Push as much authority down and out to the front lines of your company as possible.

Communication

Communication is of extreme importance in company cultures. Recall in our definition of culture, communication is a way that beliefs, behaviors, and values spread and get replicated.

The leadership must establish by example how communication is handled in the company. Some communication is natural and informal, emerging organically from how people work together. In knowledge work environments, it is important to foster and encourage this informal form of communication. This can be managed through design of the workspace or scheduling time for informal collaboration and social activities.

At the same time, some communication must be very structured and formalized. For example, company announcements must be handled with care and precision. Employees will always treat formal communication with more weight. In the absence of clear information, people tend to substitute fear and doubt even in the most jovial of company environments. So more information, sooner, is better than less, given later.

Written communication must be executed with great care. Certainly this is true with email. But even chat or virtual meeting communication must be managed with thoughtfulness and delicacy, particularly if it's coming from more senior team members.

In meetings it is sometimes unclear whether the purpose of the meeting is to present information, brainstorm, or make a decision. Be sure to make that clear for everyone present at the beginning.

Communication about new hires and transitions out of the company must also be handled with care and respect for everyone involved.

In fact, it's worth separating hiring patterns out explicitly. It is vital to a startup's success to get this right.

Hiring & On-boarding

New hires should be announced and welcomed. No team member should ever be uncertain about who their manager is, what their responsibilities are, and how well they are doing at executing on those responsibilities.

Employees should take part in setting their own goals. It should be very clear how their personal goals align with those of the company, and exactly how they will be measured.

The event of someone leaving your company should be handled delicately. Whether it is amicable or hostile, you should treat the employee that is leaving with as much dignity and respect as possible. You should also make sure to manage the expectations of the remaining team. No matter what, someone will be uncomfortable and nervous if a valued team member leaves for any reason. You have to control the narrative or people will fill their uncertainty with fear and unwarranted assumptions.

Transparency

Transparency, if you choose to embrace it as one of your values, is a big commitment. If you say you value transparency, and you fail to deliver on it, you will severely damage your reputation as a leader. That damage is extremely difficult to repair.

If transparency is to be one of your values, you must spend extra time managing the narrative for all inter-company communication. You must be prepared to answer awkward questions with honesty and respect.

One key area of transparency in communication is the financial health of the company. Many founders struggle with this aspect. They sometimes assume that employees lack the maturity and experience to be able to handle the truth about company finance. Such an assumption really sells people short. In my experience (and I have been on both sides of this conversation more than once), it is much better to be transparent about financial health than to pretend everything is great when it's not. They will find out eventually.

Feedback

Ask for feedback from your team about your performance as a leader. It will be difficult for you and for them at first. But it will make you a better leader and make them a better team. Ask for feedback on company strategy and objectives as well. If you've hired smart people, valuable feedback can come from anyone. Don't be afraid to hear it.

Don't ask for feedback on a public forum unless you are prepared to field any possible question from your team. Don't shut people down publicly in front of their peers. Take them aside and talk directly and honestly about your concern.

...

I've provided here a sizable set of patterns and suggestions on how to structure your startup to increase the chances that you'll develop a good strong culture.

It's worth noting here, in case it hasn't occurred to you yet, that culture is an emergent property of organization. You can't operate on it directly. The best you can do is to put the right people, structure, process, and space in place, and then regularly monitor your culture for signs of toxicity.

CONCLUSION

So, here we are, at the end of our little journey together, at least for now. But the beginning of a wild new adventure for you, I hope!

If this book were a school, this chapter would be the graduation commencement speech. So, I'll share some parting words of wisdom meant to send you on your way, inspired and hopeful.

First, in a little bit of a "meta" vein, I'll share something about the process of writing a book itself.

A book project is not unlike doing a startup. It's an exercise in creating something that is very personal to you, an original concept or vision, and sending it out into the world, to be praised or pilloried by the public. It feels a bit like walking around without skin.

With startups, you have your big idea that you carry around safely cushioned in the privacy of your own head. It's only when you dare to share the idea with other people that you very quickly realize it is not as perfect and shiny as you had first imagined. It can be painful sharing something so personal for others to critique.

I think that's why, even in this age of agile and lean startup content everywhere you turn, so many founders still wait too long before getting early and honest feedback from the market. It takes a very resilient attitude, and a growth mindset, frankly, to be able to learn from the world's feedback, to not take it personally. But you have to adapt your vision to meet the world where it really is. After all, why do a startup if nobody wants what you sell? Why write a book if no one will read it?

I have taken a very Lean Startup approach to writing this book. I posted each chapter on my blog as I wrote it, and invited feedback from readers. I expected the feedback process to be painful, but really it was quite the opposite. Early readers were incredibly supportive, offering suggestions for content, changes to wording for readability, and pushing for more depth and breadth in the topics covered.

What that tells me is that holding back your work from the public eye until it is "perfect" and "presentable" is only cheating yourself out of an opportunity for growth and development.

Despite my fear and insecurity, which everyone feels at one time or another, the openness and transparency with which I wrote this work, the early exposure to public scrutiny to which I subjected it, served to greatly improve the outcome. Trust me: the book I had in my head at the beginning of this process was nowhere near as good as this one has turned out to be.

It took me two years to finish it. A lot has happened in that time. I have changed jobs twice, and engaged in over a dozen side consulting projects. I started, tested, and abandoned five or six different side business ideas. I also greatly ramped up my public speaking practice, testing content from the book in front of live audiences. All of it has affected the outcome in positive ways.

So, even before I push the "publish" button, I consider this work a success, one that you, dear reader, have already contributed to. So thank you.

Now let's talk about failure.

The main work room in the RadicalFusion office was a bright, airy ground level unit in a renovated Victorian in Oakland's Preservation Park. It was early Autumn in 2011, and the sun was shining. The room was about 800 square feet, occupied with IKEA desks sporting Mac laptops and brightly colored office chairs.

It was 11am. Our seven remaining employees stood gathered around me in a semi-circle. I proceeded to make the most painful and awkward announcement I have ever had to give. We were completely out of cash, with no immediate prospects on the horizon. After almost a decade of building this company, we were forced to close the doors for good.

What had happened? Why had things that had held together for ten years so suddenly fallen apart? There were a lot of contributing circumstances, but in the intervening 5 years since that moment, I have boiled it down to two specific and concrete lessons.

First, I had naively gambled the company on executing a pivot from a web development agency into a product company. Anyone in the services business knows it is extremely hard to scale. You are always balancing the effort of bringing in work with that of recruiting the talent to do it. That's true in any company, but in service it's particularly tricky because your whole value proposition is the people, their skills and availability. It's very hard to balance demand and supply, especially when almost every project is custom work.

Some service businesses have successfully executed this pivot, 37 Signals perhaps the most famous example. It's not impossible. But in our case, we simply did not have enough market validation that we could sell the product we were building. I had by now heard of Customer Development, and the Lean Startup book had just been published. But we had already over-engineered our product, and allocated critical team resources to it for months--with no customers lined up yet--by the time I learned what an MVP was!

Second, I had taken my eye off of sales, distracted by the desire to build this product. While I allocated team effort to building it, accruing payroll expense with no client work to cover their costs (in retrospect, an idiotic mistake), I at least should have been out hustling for more client work to balance things out. But I wasn't. I was so consumed by the pivot we were trying to pull off, so engrossed in designing the perfect product, that when I finally came up for air it was too late. I was a day late and a dollar short on this one, and the results were disaster.

We were very good at software development at RadicalFusion. I knew how to build software, how recruit, train, and manage engineers, and how to translate client requirements into working technology products. But my focus was on the building, not the selling.

So while the first twelve years of my career were focused on technology, the last five have been focused on business. In that time, I have taught myself sales and content marketing, and how to simulate financial models and calculate risk. I learned how to conduct customer interviews and validate business ideas with little or even no coding. And the driving motivator to learn these things was that experience of being forced by circumstances of my own creation to close down our beloved company.

So, we've talked about success, and how getting early and honest feedback is a critical component to being successful. We've talked about failure, and underscored how avoiding early and honest feedback can destroy your company. Finally, let's talk about the leadership that makes the difference.

The collapse of RadicalFusion was an extremely traumatic lesson for me, and it taught me a lot about leadership, particularly what was good and not so good of my own. And I have had the opportunity in the last five years to work with, and observe, many other leaders. I have been paid respectable sums to give my advice to founders who are just starting out, founders who have teams of 5 to 10 employees, founders who run companies of 200 employees or more, and even directors and vice presidents in charge of product divisions at major enterprises.

I have attempted in this book to impart the advice I give to them, to outline the patterns of leadership that successful founders use to build healthy and growing startup companies.

Above all else, the best startup leaders can articulate a strong and clear vision for the company. Every decision should be evaluated based on whether it moves the company closer to achieving that vision.

They design and evolve a relatively simple strategy for how the company plans to navigate from an initial MVP to the longer term vision. They ensure that everyone on the team understands the company's strategy, and their role in it.

They use a detailed and accurate economic framework to model the company's business. They are able to make product and strategy adjustments that focus on the best overall economic outcome.

They choose to focus on the metrics that matter, and avoid those that are just background noise. They are able to explain and justify their rationale for these metrics, including how the company will move from the empathy, to the stickiness, and finally growth stages of startup development.

They understand risk and prioritization. They appreciate the tradeoffs required to build a company under conditions of extreme uncertainty.

They make sure the company is solving the right problem. They validate this by collecting early and regular feedback from paying customers.

They respect the flow of work, the system of constraints that enable that flow, and the feedback mechanisms necessary to increase it. Leaders are either directly adding value to the product or they get out of the way and let the team do its job.

They build excellent teams, not of divas, ninjas, and rockstars, but of skilled and committed team members who know how to give and get honest and direct feedback. Leaders delegate effectively and respect the relative autonomy of their teams.

They turn competition into an advantage. They know the difference between a direct competitor and a potential partner. They are focused on strengthening their company's differentiators by building something the market wants and doing it faster than everyone else.

They raise money only when they need it. They employ capital only when it fuels expansion into an already validated market.

They build an open, transparent, and supportive culture. They take communication and feedback seriously. They own their mistakes, and lead by setting the first example.

These are the patterns of successful startups. And if you follow them, if you really commit yourself to the principles we've discussed, you will greatly increase your chances of success.

Good luck. I'll be here if you need me.

BIBLIOGRAPHY

Anderson, David J. (2010). Kanban: Successful Evolutionary Change For Your Technology Business. Blue Hole Press. Sequim, WA.

Baghai M, Coley S, White D. (2000). The Alchemy of Growth, Practical Insights for Building the Enduring Enterprise. Da Capo Press. Cambridge, MA.

Beck, Kent with Cynthia Andres. (1999, 2005). Extreme Programming Explained, Second Edition. Embrace Change. Addison-Wesley. Boston, MA.

Blank, Steve. (2003). Four Steps to the Epiphany. cafepress.com

Constable, Giff. (2014). Talking to Humans. Self-published.

Croll, Alistair, Yoskovitz, Benjamin (2013). Lean Analytics: Use Data to Build a Better Startup Faster. O'Reilly Media. Sebastopol, CA.

Deming, William Edwards. (2000). Out of the Crisis. MIT Press. Cambridge, MA.

Goldratt, Eli. (1984). The Goal. North River Press. Great Barrington, MA.

Kaplan, Robert Steven. (2011). What To Ask The Person In The Mirror. Harvard Business Review Press. Cambridge, MA.

Kromer, Tristan. Grasshopper Herder Blog. http://grasshopperherder.com Accessed July, 2015.

Reinertsen, Donald. (2009). Flow: Principles of Lean Product Development. Celeritas Publishing. Redondo Beach, CA

Reis, Eric. (2011). The Lean Startup. Crown Business Press. New York, NY.

ABOUT THE AUTHOR

Sam has helped numerous technology product teams to be successful and deliver meaningfully for their business. He participated directly in six startups, and has coached and advised countless others. He has long been an active member of the Agile and Lean Startup communities of practice in the Bay Area. He has significant hands-on experience developing a wide variety of software products.

Sam's latest venture is Blackwillow Studios, where he and his team build popup incubators for large companies and nonprofit organizations.

You can find him on Twitter at @sammcafee and you can get access to more resources based on this book at http://startuppatternsbook.com.

Made in the USA
San Bernardino, CA
09 November 2019